TEACHER'S PET PUBLICATIONS

PUZZLE PACK
for
Homecoming

based on the book by
Cynthia Voigt

Written by
William T. Collins

© 2005 Teacher's Pet Publications
All Rights Reserved

The materials in this packet are copyrighted
by Teacher's Pet Publications, Inc.

These pages may be duplicated by the purchaser
for use in the purchaser's own classroom.

Copying any of these materials and distributing them
for any other purpose is a violation of the copyright laws.

© 2005 Teacher's Pet Publications, Inc.
www.tpet.com

INTRODUCTION
If you already own the LitPlan for this title, this Puzzle Pack will refresh your Unit Resource Materials and Vocabulary Resource Materials sections plus give you additional materials you can substitute into the tests. If you do not already have a complete LitPlan, these pages will give you some supplemental materials to use with your own plan. There are two main groups of materials: one set for unit words (such as characters' names, symbols, places, etc.) and one set for vocabulary words associated with the book.

WORD LIST
There is a word list for both the unit words and the vocabulary words. These lists show you which words are being used in the materials and the clues or definitions being used for those words. You may want to give students a word list with clues/definitions to help them, or you may want students to only have a word list (without clues/definitions) if you want them to work a little harder. Both are available for duplication. The word lists can also be your "calling key" for the bingo games.

FILL IN THE BLANK AND MATCHING
There are 4 each of the fill in the blank and matching worksheets for both the unit and vocabulary words. These pages can be used either as extra worksheets for students or as objective parts of a unit test. They can be done individually if students need extra help or as a whole class activity to review the material covered.

MAGIC SQUARES
The magic squares not only reinforce the material covered but also work on reasoning and math skills. Many teachers have told us that their students really enjoy doing these!

WORD SEARCH PUZZLES
The word search words go in all directions, as indicated on your answer keys. Two of the word search puzzles have the clues listed rather than the words. This makes the puzzle a little more difficult, but it reinforces the material better. Two word search puzzles have words only for students who find the clue puzzles too difficult.

CROSSWORD PUZZLES
Both unit and vocabulary word sections have 4 crossword puzzles.

BINGO CARDS
There are 32 individual bingo cards for the unit words and 32 individual bingo cards for the vocabulary words. You can use your word list as a "call list," calling the words at random and marking them off of your list as you go, or you could use the flash cards by cutting them apart and drawing the words at random from a hat (or box or whatever). To make a better review, you might ask for the definition and spelling of each word as you call it out–or you could call out the definitions and have students tell you the words they need to look for on the puzzle.

JUGGLE LETTERS
The vocabulary juggle letter game is intended to help students learn the spellings of the words. One sheet has the definitions listed on it as an extra help for students who need it or to reinforce the definitions if you choose to do so.

FLASH CARDS
We've included a set of vocabulary flash cards you can duplicate, cut, and fold for your students. Some teachers make a few sets for general use by the class; others make a set for each student. Some teachers duplicate them for each student and have the students cut & fold their own. You can cut out just the words and put them in a hat, have each student pick out one word and write the definition and a sentence for that word. Students then swap words and papers, with the next student adding a sentence of his own under the last one. You can have students swap as many times as you like. Each time the student will read the sentences written prior to his own and then add a sentence. You can cut out the words and definitions separately and play "I Have; Who Has?" Each student in the room draws a word and definition. The first student says, "I have (the name of the word). Who has the definition?" The student with the definition reads it then says, "I have (the name of the vocabulary word she has). Who has the definition?" The round continues until all words and definitions have been given.

Homecoming Word List

No.	Word	Clue/Definition
1.	ANNAPOLIS	The children met Jerry & Tom at a boatyard there.
2.	BICYCLE	Each child received one when Will & Claire visited the farm.
3.	BOAT	Dicey found one in the barn.
4.	BOOKS	Grandmother said her husband used these to build a wall to keep things out.
5.	BOULDER	James fell off one at Rockland State Park.
6.	BRIDGEPORT	City where Aunt Cilla lived
7.	CAR	Dicey got $57 for the sale of her mother's.
8.	CEMETERY	Where the children slept after rowing across the river
9.	CLAIRE	She ran off Mr. Rudyard & rescued the children.
10.	CRABS	The Tillerman children learn to eat these at their grandmother's house.
11.	CRISFIELD	Abigail Tillerman lives there.
12.	DANNY	The mall guard, Lou, & Edie believe Dicey is a boy named ____.
13.	DIED	Eunice told the children that Aunt Cilla had ____.
14.	FISH	Sammy caught them at Rockland State Park.
15.	GRANDMOTHER	Dicey decides to go to Crisfield to meet her ____.
16.	GRATEFUL	Dicey figures the expense of staying with cousin Eunice is the cost of always being this.
17.	GREENSLEEVES	Song Maybeth sang with Stewart
18.	JOSEPH	Father ____: Cousin Eunice's friend & spiritual counselor
19.	LIGHT	James says the only true, unchanging thing is the speed of ____.
20.	LOGAN	Eunice's last name
21.	MAP	The children ate at McDonalds and bought a __ in Fairfield.
22.	MASS	Cousin Eunice goes to this every morning at 6:30.
23.	MAYBETH	Persuades Sammy to start walking to Bridgeport
24.	MENTAL	Kind of hospital Dicey's mother is in, in Massachusetts
25.	MONEY	Lou & Edie stole this from Edie's father.
26.	MOTHER	The storekeeper in St. Michaels sounded like Dicey's ____.
27.	NUN	Cousin Eunice must abandon her plans for becoming one.
28.	PEGGY	Character in a song the children's mother taught them: ____-O
29.	RETARDED	Word Fr. Joseph applies to Maybeth in his discussion with Dicey
30.	ROCKLAND	The children ate mussels & clams at this state park.
31.	RUDYARD	He chased the children with his dogs.
32.	SAMMY	He always argues with Dicey's decisions.
33.	SOUR	Kind of expression Dicey's grandmother's picture had
34.	STEER	Jerry allows Dicey to do ____ the boat.
35.	STEWART	James stole money from him in the dormitory room.
36.	TILLERMAN	Family name for Dicey & siblings
37.	TOMATO	The children decide to make money by becoming ___ pickers.
38.	VERRICKER	Dicey's long-missing father's name: Francis ____
39.	WALLET	Dicey made Sammy return the ____ he stole that had $20 in it.
40.	WILL	He drove the children to Crisfield.
41.	WINDOWS	Dicey got a job washing them.

Homecoming Fill In The Blanks 1

_____

_____

_____

_____

_____

_____

_____

_____

_____

_____

_____

_____

_____

_____

_____

_____

_____

_____

_____

_____

1. Dicey made Sammy return the ___ he stole that had $20 in it.
2. Cousin Eunice goes to this every morning at 6:30.
3. Dicey figures the expense of staying with cousin Eunice is the cost of always being this.
4. James stole money from him in the dormitory room.
5. The children ate at McDonalds and bought a ___ in Fairfield.
6. The children decide to make money by becoming ___ pickers.
7. Cousin Eunice must abandon her plans for becoming one.
8. Dicey found one in the barn.
9. Eunice told the children that Aunt Cilla had ___.
10. Family name for Dicey & siblings
11. Dicey's long-missing father's name: Francis ___
12. She ran off Mr. Rudyard & rescued the children.
13. He drove the children to Crisfield.
14. Dicey got $57 for the sale of her mother's.
15. Father ___: Cousin Eunice's friend & spiritual counselor
16. The storekeeper in St. Michaels sounded like Dicey's ___.
17. Grandmother said her husband used these to build a wall to keep things out.
18. City where Aunt Cilla lived
19. Eunice's last name
20. Song Maybeth sang with Stewart

Homecoming Fill In The Blanks 1 Answer Key

WALLET	1. Dicey made Sammy return the ___ he stole that had $20 in it.
MASS	2. Cousin Eunice goes to this every morning at 6:30.
GRATEFUL	3. Dicey figures the expense of staying with cousin Eunice is the cost of always being this.
STEWART	4. James stole money from him in the dormitory room.
MAP	5. The children ate at McDonalds and bought a __ in Fairfield.
TOMATO	6. The children decide to make money by becoming ___ pickers.
NUN	7. Cousin Eunice must abandon her plans for becoming one.
BOAT	8. Dicey found one in the barn.
DIED	9. Eunice told the children that Aunt Cilla had ___.
TILLERMAN	10. Family name for Dicey & siblings
VERRICKER	11. Dicey's long-missing father's name: Francis ___
CLAIRE	12. She ran off Mr. Rudyard & rescued the children.
WILL	13. He drove the children to Crisfield.
CAR	14. Dicey got $57 for the sale of her mother's.
JOSEPH	15. Father ___: Cousin Eunice's friend & spiritual counselor
MOTHER	16. The storekeeper in St. Michaels sounded like Dicey's ___.
BOOKS	17. Grandmother said her husband used these to build a wall to keep things out.
BRIDGEPORT	18. City where Aunt Cilla lived
LOGAN	19. Eunice's last name
GREENSLEEVES	20. Song Maybeth sang with Stewart

Homecoming Fill In The Blanks 2

_____

1. The storekeeper in St. Michaels sounded like Dicey's ___.
2. Dicey's long-missing father's name: Francis ___
3. Father ___: Cousin Eunice's friend & spiritual counselor
4. Sammy caught them at Rockland State Park.
5. He chased the children with his dogs.
6. Eunice's last name
7. Each child received one when Will & Claire visited the farm.
8. The mall guard, Lou, & Edie believe Dicey is a boy named ____.
9. City where Aunt Cilla lived
10. Grandmother said her husband used these to build a wall to keep things out.
11. Word Fr. Joseph applies to Maybeth in his discussion with Dicey
12. Family name for Dicey & siblings
13. Cousin Eunice must abandon her plans for becoming one.
14. Kind of hospital Dicey's mother is in, in Massachusetts
15. Where the children slept after rowing across the river
16. The Tillerman children learn to eat these at their grandmother's house.
17. Dicey found one in the barn.
18. Song Maybeth sang with Stewart
19. The children met Jerry & Tom at a boatyard there.
20. He always argues with Dicey's decisions.

Homecoming Fill In The Blanks 2 Answer Key

MOTHER	1. The storekeeper in St. Michaels sounded like Dicey's ___.
VERRICKER	2. Dicey's long-missing father's name: Francis ___
JOSEPH	3. Father ___: Cousin Eunice's friend & spiritual counselor
FISH	4. Sammy caught them at Rockland State Park.
RUDYARD	5. He chased the children with his dogs.
LOGAN	6. Eunice's last name
BICYCLE	7. Each child received one when Will & Claire visited the farm.
DANNY	8. The mall guard, Lou, & Edie believe Dicey is a boy named ____.
BRIDGEPORT	9. City where Aunt Cilla lived
BOOKS	10. Grandmother said her husband used these to build a wall to keep things out.
RETARDED	11. Word Fr. Joseph applies to Maybeth in his discussion with Dicey
TILLERMAN	12. Family name for Dicey & siblings
NUN	13. Cousin Eunice must abandon her plans for becoming one.
MENTAL	14. Kind of hospital Dicey's mother is in, in Massachusetts
CEMETERY	15. Where the children slept after rowing across the river
CRABS	16. The Tillerman children learn to eat these at their grandmother's house.
BOAT	17. Dicey found one in the barn.
GREENSLEEVES	18. Song Maybeth sang with Stewart
ANNAPOLIS	19. The children met Jerry & Tom at a boatyard there.
SAMMY	20. He always argues with Dicey's decisions.

Homecoming Fill In The Blanks 3

_____

_____

_____

_____

_____

_____

_____

_____

_____

_____

_____

_____

_____

_____

_____

_____

_____

_____

_____

_____

1. Family name for Dicey & siblings
2. City where Aunt Cilla lived
3. Abigail Tillerman lives there.
4. The mall guard, Lou, & Edie believe Dicey is a boy named ____.
5. Grandmother said her husband used these to build a wall to keep things out.
6. Kind of expression Dicey's grandmother's picture had
7. Cousin Eunice goes to this every morning at 6:30.
8. Dicey made Sammy return the ___ he stole that had $20 in it.
9. James stole money from him in the dormitory room.
10. Eunice's last name
11. Kind of hospital Dicey's mother is in, in Massachusetts
12. Dicey figures the expense of staying with cousin Eunice is the cost of always being this.
13. James says the only true, unchanging thing is the speed of ____.
14. Dicey got a job washing them.
15. James fell off one at Rockland State Park.
16. Dicey decides to go to Crisfield to meet her ____.
17. She ran off Mr. Rudyard & rescued the children.
18. Jerry allows Dicey to do ___ the boat.
19. The children decide to make money by becoming ___ pickers.
20. The children met Jerry & Tom at a boatyard there.

Homecoming Fill In The Blanks 3 Answer Key

TILLERMAN	1. Family name for Dicey & siblings
BRIDGEPORT	2. City where Aunt Cilla lived
CRISFIELD	3. Abigail Tillerman lives there.
DANNY	4. The mall guard, Lou, & Edie believe Dicey is a boy named ____.
BOOKS	5. Grandmother said her husband used these to build a wall to keep things out.
SOUR	6. Kind of expression Dicey's grandmother's picture had
MASS	7. Cousin Eunice goes to this every morning at 6:30.
WALLET	8. Dicey made Sammy return the ___ he stole that had $20 in it.
STEWART	9. James stole money from him in the dormitory room.
LOGAN	10. Eunice's last name
MENTAL	11. Kind of hospital Dicey's mother is in, in Massachusetts
GRATEFUL	12. Dicey figures the expense of staying with cousin Eunice is the cost of always being this.
LIGHT	13. James says the only true, unchanging thing is the speed of ___.
WINDOWS	14. Dicey got a job washing them.
BOULDER	15. James fell off one at Rockland State Park.
GRANDMOTHER	16. Dicey decides to go to Crisfield to meet her ___.
CLAIRE	17. She ran off Mr. Rudyard & rescued the children.
STEER	18. Jerry allows Dicey to do ___ the boat.
TOMATO	19. The children decide to make money by becoming ___ pickers.
ANNAPOLIS	20. The children met Jerry & Tom at a boatyard there.

Homecoming Fill In The Blanks 4

_____

_____

_____

_____

_____

_____

_____

_____

_____

_____

_____

_____

_____

_____

_____

_____

_____

_____

_____

_____

1. Character in a song the children's mother taught them: ___-O
2. City where Aunt Cilla lived
3. Dicey got $57 for the sale of her mother's.
4. Word Fr. Joseph applies to Maybeth in his discussion with Dicey
5. Grandmother said her husband used these to build a wall to keep things out.
6. Dicey figures the expense of staying with cousin Eunice is the cost of always being this.
7. James says the only true, unchanging thing is the speed of ___.
8. Kind of hospital Dicey's mother is in, in Massachusetts
9. The children ate mussels & clams at this state park.
10. Dicey got a job washing them.
11. He always argues with Dicey's decisions.
12. Each child received one when Will & Claire visited the farm.
13. Jerry allows Dicey to do ___ the boat.
14. Where the children slept after rowing across the river
15. Eunice's last name
16. Father ___: Cousin Eunice's friend & spiritual counselor
17. Sammy caught them at Rockland State Park.
18. Song Maybeth sang with Stewart
19. He chased the children with his dogs.
20. Cousin Eunice goes to this every morning at 6:30.

Homecoming Fill In The Blanks 4 Answer Key

PEGGY	1. Character in a song the children's mother taught them: ___-O
BRIDGEPORT	2. City where Aunt Cilla lived
CAR	3. Dicey got $57 for the sale of her mother's.
RETARDED	4. Word Fr. Joseph applies to Maybeth in his discussion with Dicey
BOOKS	5. Grandmother said her husband used these to build a wall to keep things out.
GRATEFUL	6. Dicey figures the expense of staying with cousin Eunice is the cost of always being this.
LIGHT	7. James says the only true, unchanging thing is the speed of ___.
MENTAL	8. Kind of hospital Dicey's mother is in, in Massachusetts
ROCKLAND	9. The children ate mussels & clams at this state park.
WINDOWS	10. Dicey got a job washing them.
SAMMY	11. He always argues with Dicey's decisions.
BICYCLE	12. Each child received one when Will & Claire visited the farm.
STEER	13. Jerry allows Dicey to do ___ the boat.
CEMETERY	14. Where the children slept after rowing across the river
LOGAN	15. Eunice's last name
JOSEPH	16. Father ___: Cousin Eunice's friend & spiritual counselor
FISH	17. Sammy caught them at Rockland State Park.
GREENSLEEVES	18. Song Maybeth sang with Stewart
RUDYARD	19. He chased the children with his dogs.
MASS	20. Cousin Eunice goes to this every morning at 6:30.

Homecoming Matching 1

___ 1. TILLERMAN   A. Cousin Eunice goes to this every morning at 6:30.
___ 2. WINDOWS   B. The children met Jerry & Tom at a boatyard there.
___ 3. ANNAPOLIS   C. Family name for Dicey & siblings
___ 4. NUN   D. Abigail Tillerman lives there.
___ 5. CRISFIELD   E. Dicey got a job washing them.
___ 6. RETARDED   F. Word Fr. Joseph applies to Maybeth in his discussion with Dicey
___ 7. WALLET   G. Song Maybeth sang with Stewart
___ 8. MONEY   H. Dicey got $57 for the sale of her mother's.
___ 9. STEWART   I. Dicey made Sammy return the ___ he stole that had $20 in it.
___ 10. BOAT   J. Grandmother said her husband used these to build a wall to keep things out.
___ 11. MOTHER   K. The storekeeper in St. Michaels sounded like Dicey's ___.
___ 12. ROCKLAND   L. He always argues with Dicey's decisions.
___ 13. MASS   M. Persuades Sammy to start walking to Bridgeport
___ 14. GREENSLEEVES   N. Lou & Edie stole this from Edie's father.
___ 15. CAR   O. Each child received one when Will & Claire visited the farm.
___ 16. MAYBETH   P. James stole money from him in the dormitory room.
___ 17. WILL   Q. Jerry allows Dicey to do ___ the boat.
___ 18. SAMMY   R. James says the only true, unchanging thing is the speed of ___.
___ 19. PEGGY   S. The children ate mussels & clams at this state park.
___ 20. LIGHT   T. He drove the children to Crisfield.
___ 21. BICYCLE   U. City where Aunt Cilla lived
___ 22. BRIDGEPORT   V. Dicey found one in the barn.
___ 23. STEER   W. Dicey decides to go to Crisfield to meet her ___.
___ 24. BOOKS   X. Character in a song the children's mother taught them: ___-O
___ 25. GRANDMOTHER   Y. Cousin Eunice must abandon her plans for becoming one.

Homecoming Matching 1 Answer Key

C - 1. TILLERMAN	A. Cousin Eunice goes to this every morning at 6:30.
E - 2. WINDOWS	B. The children met Jerry & Tom at a boatyard there.
B - 3. ANNAPOLIS	C. Family name for Dicey & siblings
Y - 4. NUN	D. Abigail Tillerman lives there.
D - 5. CRISFIELD	E. Dicey got a job washing them.
F - 6. RETARDED	F. Word Fr. Joseph applies to Maybeth in his discussion with Dicey
I - 7. WALLET	G. Song Maybeth sang with Stewart
N - 8. MONEY	H. Dicey got $57 for the sale of her mother's.
P - 9. STEWART	I. Dicey made Sammy return the ___ he stole that had $20 in it.
V - 10. BOAT	J. Grandmother said her husband used these to build a wall to keep things out.
K - 11. MOTHER	K. The storekeeper in St. Michaels sounded like Dicey's ___.
S - 12. ROCKLAND	L. He always argues with Dicey's decisions.
A - 13. MASS	M. Persuades Sammy to start walking to Bridgeport
G - 14. GREENSLEEVES	N. Lou & Edie stole this from Edie's father.
H - 15. CAR	O. Each child received one when Will & Claire visited the farm.
M - 16. MAYBETH	P. James stole money from him in the dormitory room.
T - 17. WILL	Q. Jerry allows Dicey to do ___ the boat.
L - 18. SAMMY	R. James says the only true, unchanging thing is the speed of ___.
X - 19. PEGGY	S. The children ate mussels & clams at this state park.
R - 20. LIGHT	T. He drove the children to Crisfield.
O - 21. BICYCLE	U. City where Aunt Cilla lived
U - 22. BRIDGEPORT	V. Dicey found one in the barn.
Q - 23. STEER	W. Dicey decides to go to Crisfield to meet her ___.
J - 24. BOOKS	X. Character in a song the children's mother taught them: ___-O
W - 25. GRANDMOTHER	Y. Cousin Eunice must abandon her plans for becoming one.

Homecoming Matching 2

___ 1. BOULDER A. The children met Jerry & Tom at a boatyard there.
___ 2. MONEY B. Eunice's last name
___ 3. VERRICKER C. Kind of hospital Dicey's mother is in, in Massachusetts
___ 4. FISH D. Dicey got $57 for the sale of her mother's.
___ 5. STEER E. Abigail Tillerman lives there.
___ 6. CRISFIELD F. Dicey made Sammy return the ___ he stole that had $20 in it.
___ 7. MENTAL G. Lou & Edie stole this from Edie's father.
___ 8. TILLERMAN H. He always argues with Dicey's decisions.
___ 9. WILL I. James stole money from him in the dormitory room.
___ 10. GRATEFUL J. The children ate mussels & clams at this state park.
___ 11. DANNY K. James fell off one at Rockland State Park.
___ 12. RETARDED L. Sammy caught them at Rockland State Park.
___ 13. DIED M. He drove the children to Crisfield.
___ 14. NUN N. Dicey's long-missing father's name: Francis ___
___ 15. CAR O. The mall guard, Lou, & Edie believe Dicey is a boy named ___.
___ 16. ANNAPOLIS P. Word Fr. Joseph applies to Maybeth in his discussion with Dicey
___ 17. MOTHER Q. Cousin Eunice goes to this every morning at 6:30.
___ 18. SAMMY R. Grandmother said her husband used these to build a wall to keep things out.
___ 19. BICYCLE S. Each child received one when Will & Claire visited the farm.
___ 20. STEWART T. Jerry allows Dicey to do ___ the boat.
___ 21. MASS U. Eunice told the children that Aunt Cilla had ___.
___ 22. ROCKLAND V. Family name for Dicey & siblings
___ 23. LOGAN W. The storekeeper in St. Michaels sounded like Dicey's ___.
___ 24. WALLET X. Cousin Eunice must abandon her plans for becoming one.
___ 25. BOOKS Y. Dicey figures the expense of staying with cousin Eunice is the cost of always being this.

Homecoming Matching 2 Answer Key

K - 1. BOULDER	A. The children met Jerry & Tom at a boatyard there.
G - 2. MONEY	B. Eunice's last name
N - 3. VERRICKER	C. Kind of hospital Dicey's mother is in, in Massachusetts
L - 4. FISH	D. Dicey got $57 for the sale of her mother's.
T - 5. STEER	E. Abigail Tillerman lives there.
E - 6. CRISFIELD	F. Dicey made Sammy return the ___ he stole that had $20 in it.
C - 7. MENTAL	G. Lou & Edie stole this from Edie's father.
V - 8. TILLERMAN	H. He always argues with Dicey's decisions.
M - 9. WILL	I. James stole money from him in the dormitory room.
Y - 10. GRATEFUL	J. The children ate mussels & clams at this state park.
O - 11. DANNY	K. James fell off one at Rockland State Park.
P - 12. RETARDED	L. Sammy caught them at Rockland State Park.
U - 13. DIED	M. He drove the children to Crisfield.
X - 14. NUN	N. Dicey's long-missing father's name: Francis ___
D - 15. CAR	O. The mall guard, Lou, & Edie believe Dicey is a boy named ___.
A - 16. ANNAPOLIS	P. Word Fr. Joseph applies to Maybeth in his discussion with Dicey
W - 17. MOTHER	Q. Cousin Eunice goes to this every morning at 6:30.
H - 18. SAMMY	R. Grandmother said her husband used these to build a wall to keep things out.
S - 19. BICYCLE	S. Each child received one when Will & Claire visited the farm.
I - 20. STEWART	T. Jerry allows Dicey to do ___ the boat.
Q - 21. MASS	U. Eunice told the children that Aunt Cilla had ___.
J - 22. ROCKLAND	V. Family name for Dicey & siblings
B - 23. LOGAN	W. The storekeeper in St. Michaels sounded like Dicey's ___.
F - 24. WALLET	X. Cousin Eunice must abandon her plans for becoming one.
R - 25. BOOKS	Y. Dicey figures the expense of staying with cousin Eunice is the cost of always being this.

Homecoming Matching 3

___ 1. STEWART   A. Dicey got $57 for the sale of her mother's.
___ 2. LIGHT   B. Eunice's last name
___ 3. DANNY   C. Family name for Dicey & siblings
___ 4. ROCKLAND   D. The storekeeper in St. Michaels sounded like Dicey's ___.
___ 5. MAYBETH   E. Song Maybeth sang with Stewart
___ 6. MASS   F. The Tillerman children learn to eat these at their grandmother's house.
___ 7. GREENSLEEVES   G. Dicey decides to go to Crisfield to meet her ___.
___ 8. NUN   H. The children ate mussels & clams at this state park.
___ 9. VERRICKER   I. Dicey figures the expense of staying with cousin Eunice is the cost of always being this.
___10. SOUR   J. The mall guard, Lou, & Edie believe Dicey is a boy named ____.
___11. WILL   K. James says the only true, unchanging thing is the speed of ___.
___12. CAR   L. James fell off one at Rockland State Park.
___13. BRIDGEPORT   M. City where Aunt Cilla lived
___14. GRATEFUL   N. James stole money from him in the dormitory room.
___15. ANNAPOLIS   O. Dicey's long-missing father's name: Francis ___
___16. STEER   P. Kind of expression Dicey's grandmother's picture had
___17. BOULDER   Q. The children met Jerry & Tom at a boatyard there.
___18. MOTHER   R. Jerry allows Dicey to do ___ the boat.
___19. BOAT   S. He drove the children to Crisfield.
___20. TILLERMAN   T. Word Fr. Joseph applies to Maybeth in his discussion with Dicey
___21. CRABS   U. Dicey found one in the barn.
___22. LOGAN   V. Cousin Eunice goes to this every morning at 6:30.
___23. BOOKS   W. Cousin Eunice must abandon her plans for becoming one.
___24. GRANDMOTHER   X. Grandmother said her husband used these to build a wall to keep things out.
___25. RETARDED   Y. Persuades Sammy to start walking to Bridgeport

Homecoming Matching 3 Answer Key

N - 1. STEWART
K - 2. LIGHT
J - 3. DANNY
H - 4. ROCKLAND
Y - 5. MAYBETH
V - 6. MASS
E - 7. GREENSLEEVES
W - 8. NUN
O - 9. VERRICKER
P - 10. SOUR
S - 11. WILL
A - 12. CAR
M - 13. BRIDGEPORT
I - 14. GRATEFUL
Q - 15. ANNAPOLIS
R - 16. STEER
L - 17. BOULDER
D - 18. MOTHER
U - 19. BOAT
C - 20. TILLERMAN
F - 21. CRABS
B - 22. LOGAN
X - 23. BOOKS
G - 24. GRANDMOTHER
T - 25. RETARDED

A. Dicey got $57 for the sale of her mother's.
B. Eunice's last name
C. Family name for Dicey & siblings
D. The storekeeper in St. Michaels sounded like Dicey's ___.
E. Song Maybeth sang with Stewart
F. The Tillerman children learn to eat these at their grandmother's house.
G. Dicey decides to go to Crisfield to meet her ___.
H. The children ate mussels & clams at this state park.
I. Dicey figures the expense of staying with cousin Eunice is the cost of always being this.
J. The mall guard, Lou, & Edie believe Dicey is a boy named ___.
K. James says the only true, unchanging thing is the speed of ___.
L. James fell off one at Rockland State Park.
M. City where Aunt Cilla lived
N. James stole money from him in the dormitory room.
O. Dicey's long-missing father's name: Francis ___
P. Kind of expression Dicey's grandmother's picture had
Q. The children met Jerry & Tom at a boatyard there.
R. Jerry allows Dicey to do ___ the boat.
S. He drove the children to Crisfield.
T. Word Fr. Joseph applies to Maybeth in his discussion with Dicey
U. Dicey found one in the barn.
V. Cousin Eunice goes to this every morning at 6:30.
W. Cousin Eunice must abandon her plans for becoming one.
X. Grandmother said her husband used these to build a wall to keep things out.
Y. Persuades Sammy to start walking to Bridgeport

Homecoming Matching 4

___ 1. MONEY
___ 2. GRANDMOTHER
___ 3. BRIDGEPORT
___ 4. SAMMY
___ 5. PEGGY
___ 6. MASS
___ 7. JOSEPH
___ 8. VERRICKER
___ 9. RUDYARD
___ 10. WINDOWS
___ 11. MAYBETH
___ 12. FISH
___ 13. BOAT
___ 14. GREENSLEEVES
___ 15. STEWART
___ 16. LOGAN
___ 17. GRATEFUL
___ 18. RETARDED
___ 19. SOUR
___ 20. CRISFIELD
___ 21. STEER
___ 22. NUN
___ 23. CAR
___ 24. BOULDER
___ 25. TOMATO

A. Song Maybeth sang with Stewart
B. City where Aunt Cilla lived
C. Sammy caught them at Rockland State Park.
D. Abigail Tillerman lives there.
E. James stole money from him in the dormitory room.
F. Cousin Eunice must abandon her plans for becoming one.
G. The children decide to make money by becoming ___ pickers.
H. Word Fr. Joseph applies to Maybeth in his discussion with Dicey
I. Dicey got $57 for the sale of her mother's.
J. Dicey decides to go to Crisfield to meet her ___.
K. James fell off one at Rockland State Park.
L. He chased the children with his dogs.
M. Father ___: Cousin Eunice's friend & spiritual counselor
N. Dicey found one in the barn.
O. Dicey got a job washing them.
P. Dicey figures the expense of staying with cousin Eunice is the cost of always being this.
Q. Kind of expression Dicey's grandmother's picture had
R. Eunice's last name
S. Jerry allows Dicey to do ___ the boat.
T. Lou & Edie stole this from Edie's father.
U. Character in a song the children's mother taught them: ___-O
V. Persuades Sammy to start walking to Bridgeport
W. He always argues with Dicey's decisions.
X. Dicey's long-missing father's name: Francis ___
Y. Cousin Eunice goes to this every morning at 6:30.

Homecoming Matching 4 Answer Key

T - 1. MONEY	A. Song Maybeth sang with Stewart
J - 2. GRANDMOTHER	B. City where Aunt Cilla lived
B - 3. BRIDGEPORT	C. Sammy caught them at Rockland State Park.
W - 4. SAMMY	D. Abigail Tillerman lives there.
U - 5. PEGGY	E. James stole money from him in the dormitory room.
Y - 6. MASS	F. Cousin Eunice must abandon her plans for becoming one.
M - 7. JOSEPH	G. The children decide to make money by becoming ___ pickers.
X - 8. VERRICKER	H. Word Fr. Joseph applies to Maybeth in his discussion with Dicey
L - 9. RUDYARD	I. Dicey got $57 for the sale of her mother's.
O - 10. WINDOWS	J. Dicey decides to go to Crisfield to meet her ___.
V - 11. MAYBETH	K. James fell off one at Rockland State Park.
C - 12. FISH	L. He chased the children with his dogs.
N - 13. BOAT	M. Father ___: Cousin Eunice's friend & spiritual counselor
A - 14. GREENSLEEVES	N. Dicey found one in the barn.
E - 15. STEWART	O. Dicey got a job washing them.
R - 16. LOGAN	P. Dicey figures the expense of staying with cousin Eunice is the cost of always being this.
P - 17. GRATEFUL	Q. Kind of expression Dicey's grandmother's picture had
H - 18. RETARDED	R. Eunice's last name
Q - 19. SOUR	S. Jerry allows Dicey to do ___ the boat.
D - 20. CRISFIELD	T. Lou & Edie stole this from Edie's father.
S - 21. STEER	U. Character in a song the children's mother taught them: ___-O
F - 22. NUN	V. Persuades Sammy to start walking to Bridgeport
I - 23. CAR	W. He always argues with Dicey's decisions.
K - 24. BOULDER	X. Dicey's long-missing father's name: Francis ___
G - 25. TOMATO	Y. Cousin Eunice goes to this every morning at 6:30.

Homecoming Magic Squares 1

Match the definition with the vocabulary word. Put your answers in the magic squares below. When your answers are correct, all columns and rows will add to the same number.

A. MONEY
B. BOOKS
C. CRABS
D. JOSEPH
E. RETARDED
F. TOMATO
G. NUN
H. PEGGY
I. ANNAPOLIS
J. TILLERMAN
K. VERRICKER
L. STEER
M. WINDOWS
N. GRANDMOTHER
O. MAP
P. BOAT

1. The children ate at McDonalds and bought a ___ in Fairfield.
2. Father ___: Cousin Eunice's friend & spiritual counselor
3. Family name for Dicey & siblings
4. Word Fr. Joseph applies to Maybeth in his discussion with Dicey
5. The children met Jerry & Tom at a boatyard there.
6. The children decide to make money by becoming ___ pickers.
7. Dicey found one in the barn.
8. The Tillerman children learn to eat these at their grandmother's house.
9. Character in a song the children's mother taught them: ___-O
10. Dicey's long-missing father's name: Francis ___
11. Lou & Edie stole this from Edie's father.
12. Dicey decides to go to Crisfield to meet her ___.
13. Grandmother said her husband used these to build a wall to keep things out.
14. Dicey got a job washing them.
15. Cousin Eunice must abandon her plans for becoming one.
16. Jerry allows Dicey to do ___ the boat.

A=	B=	C=	D=
E=	F=	G=	H=
I=	J=	K=	L=
M=	N=	O=	P=

Homecoming Magic Squares 1 Answer Key

Match the definition with the vocabulary word. Put your answers in the magic squares below. When your answers are correct, all columns and rows will add to the same number.

A. MONEY
B. BOOKS
C. CRABS
D. JOSEPH
E. RETARDED
F. TOMATO
G. NUN
H. PEGGY
I. ANNAPOLIS
J. TILLERMAN
K. VERRICKER
L. STEER
M. WINDOWS
N. GRANDMOTHER
O. MAP
P. BOAT

1. The children ate at McDonalds and bought a __ in Fairfield.
2. Father ___: Cousin Eunice's friend & spiritual counselor
3. Family name for Dicey & siblings
4. Word Fr. Joseph applies to Maybeth in his discussion with Dicey
5. The children met Jerry & Tom at a boatyard there.
6. The children decide to make money by becoming ___ pickers.
7. Dicey found one in the barn.
8. The Tillerman children learn to eat these at their grandmother's house.
9. Character in a song the children's mother taught them: ___-O
10. Dicey's long-missing father's name: Francis ___
11. Lou & Edie stole this from Edie's father.
12. Dicey decides to go to Crisfield to meet her ___.
13. Grandmother said her husband used these to build a wall to keep things out.
14. Dicey got a job washing them.
15. Cousin Eunice must abandon her plans for becoming one.
16. Jerry allows Dicey to do ___ the boat.

A=11	B=13	C=8	D=2
E=4	F=6	G=15	H=9
I=5	J=3	K=10	L=16
M=14	N=12	O=1	P=7

Homecoming Magic Squares 2

Match the definition with the vocabulary word. Put your answers in the magic squares below. When your answers are correct, all columns and rows will add to the same number.

A. GRATEFUL
B. BOULDER
C. RUDYARD
D. DANNY
E. MONEY
F. CAR
G. LOGAN
H. PEGGY
I. ROCKLAND
J. STEER
K. WILL
L. MENTAL
M. LIGHT
N. CRISFIELD
O. RETARDED
P. SOUR

1. Dicey figures the expense of staying with cousin Eunice is the cost of always being this.
2. Abigail Tillerman lives there.
3. Jerry allows Dicey to do ___ the boat.
4. Lou & Edie stole this from Edie's father.
5. Eunice's last name
6. Kind of hospital Dicey's mother is in, in Massachusetts
7. Kind of expression Dicey's grandmother's picture had
8. He chased the children with his dogs.
9. Word Fr. Joseph applies to Maybeth in his discussion with Dicey
10. The mall guard, Lou, & Edie believe Dicey is a boy named ____.
11. Character in a song the children's mother taught them: ___-O
12. He drove the children to Crisfield.
13. The children ate mussels & clams at this state park.
14. Dicey got $57 for the sale of her mother's.
15. James fell off one at Rockland State Park.
16. James says the only true, unchanging thing is the speed of ___.

A=	B=	C=	D=
E=	F=	G=	H=
I=	J=	K=	L=
M=	N=	O=	P=

Homecoming Magic Squares 2 Answer Key

Match the definition with the vocabulary word. Put your answers in the magic squares below. When your answers are correct, all columns and rows will add to the same number.

A. GRATEFUL
B. BOULDER
C. RUDYARD
D. DANNY
E. MONEY
F. CAR
G. LOGAN
H. PEGGY
I. ROCKLAND
J. STEER
K. WILL
L. MENTAL
M. LIGHT
N. CRISFIELD
O. RETARDED
P. SOUR

1. Dicey figures the expense of staying with cousin Eunice is the cost of always being this.
2. Abigail Tillerman lives there.
3. Jerry allows Dicey to do ___ the boat.
4. Lou & Edie stole this from Edie's father.
5. Eunice's last name
6. Kind of hospital Dicey's mother is in, in Massachusetts
7. Kind of expression Dicey's grandmother's picture had
8. He chased the children with his dogs.
9. Word Fr. Joseph applies to Maybeth in his discussion with Dicey
10. The mall guard, Lou, & Edie believe Dicey is a boy named ___.
11. Character in a song the children's mother taught them: ___-O
12. He drove the children to Crisfield.
13. The children ate mussels & clams at this state park.
14. Dicey got $57 for the sale of her mother's.
15. James fell off one at Rockland State Park.
16. James says the only true, unchanging thing is the speed of ___.

A=1	B=15	C=8	D=10
E=4	F=14	G=5	H=11
I=13	J=3	K=12	L=6
M=16	N=2	O=9	P=7

Homecoming Magic Squares 3

Match the definition with the vocabulary word. Put your answers in the magic squares below. When your answers are correct, all columns and rows will add to the same number.

A. CRABS
B. BICYCLE
C. MAP
D. LIGHT
E. TOMATO
F. MASS
G. MENTAL
H. GRATEFUL
I. LOGAN
J. TILLERMAN
K. GREENSLEEVES
L. ROCKLAND
M. BRIDGEPORT
N. DANNY
O. ANNAPOLIS
P. VERRICKER

1. Dicey figures the expense of staying with cousin Eunice is the cost of always being this.
2. The Tillerman children learn to eat these at their grandmother's house.
3. Each child received one when Will & Claire visited the farm.
4. Kind of hospital Dicey's mother is in, in Massachusetts
5. Family name for Dicey & siblings
6. The children met Jerry & Tom at a boatyard there.
7. Dicey's long-missing father's name: Francis ___
8. Eunice's last name
9. Song Maybeth sang with Stewart
10. The mall guard, Lou, & Edie believe Dicey is a boy named ___.
11. City where Aunt Cilla lived
12. The children ate mussels & clams at this state park.
13. The children decide to make money by becoming ___ pickers.
14. James says the only true, unchanging thing is the speed of ___.
15. The children ate at McDonalds and bought a ___ in Fairfield.
16. Cousin Eunice goes to this every morning at 6:30.

A=	B=	C=	D=
E=	F=	G=	H=
I=	J=	K=	L=
M=	N=	O=	P=

Homecoming Magic Squares 3 Answer Key

Match the definition with the vocabulary word. Put your answers in the magic squares below. When your answers are correct, all columns and rows will add to the same number.

A. CRABS
B. BICYCLE
C. MAP
D. LIGHT
E. TOMATO
F. MASS
G. MENTAL
H. GRATEFUL
I. LOGAN
J. TILLERMAN
K. GREENSLEEVES
L. ROCKLAND
M. BRIDGEPORT
N. DANNY
O. ANNAPOLIS
P. VERRICKER

1. Dicey figures the expense of staying with cousin Eunice is the cost of always being this.
2. The Tillerman children learn to eat these at their grandmother's house.
3. Each child received one when Will & Claire visited the farm.
4. Kind of hospital Dicey's mother is in, in Massachusetts
5. Family name for Dicey & siblings
6. The children met Jerry & Tom at a boatyard there.
7. Dicey's long-missing father's name: Francis ___
8. Eunice's last name
9. Song Maybeth sang with Stewart
10. The mall guard, Lou, & Edie believe Dicey is a boy named ____.
11. City where Aunt Cilla lived
12. The children ate mussels & clams at this state park.
13. The children decide to make money by becoming ___ pickers.
14. James says the only true, unchanging thing is the speed of ___.
15. The children ate at McDonalds and bought a ___ in Fairfield.
16. Cousin Eunice goes to this every morning at 6:30.

A=2	B=3	C=15	D=14
E=13	F=16	G=4	H=1
I=8	J=5	K=9	L=12
M=11	N=10	O=6	P=7

Homecoming Magic Squares 4

Match the definition with the vocabulary word. Put your answers in the magic squares below. When your answers are correct, all columns and rows will add to the same number.

A. LIGHT
B. GREENSLEEVES
C. TILLERMAN
D. LOGAN
E. BOULDER
F. PEGGY
G. STEWART
H. NUN
I. WALLET
J. MASS
K. MENTAL
L. MONEY
M. MAYBETH
N. RETARDED
O. BOAT
P. GRANDMOTHER

1. Song Maybeth sang with Stewart
2. James stole money from him in the dormitory room.
3. Kind of hospital Dicey's mother is in, in Massachusetts
4. Word Fr. Joseph applies to Maybeth in his discussion with Dicey
5. Persuades Sammy to start walking to Bridgeport
6. Lou & Edie stole this from Edie's father.
7. Cousin Eunice must abandon her plans for becoming one.
8. James says the only true, unchanging thing is the speed of ___.
9. Dicey decides to go to Crisfield to meet her ___.
10. Dicey made Sammy return the ___ he stole that had $20 in it.
11. James fell off one at Rockland State Park.
12. Eunice's last name
13. Family name for Dicey & siblings
14. Character in a song the children's mother taught them: ___-O
15. Cousin Eunice goes to this every morning at 6:30.
16. Dicey found one in the barn.

A=	B=	C=	D=
E=	F=	G=	H=
I=	J=	K=	L=
M=	N=	O=	P=

Homecoming Magic Squares 4 Answer Key

Match the definition with the vocabulary word. Put your answers in the magic squares below. When your answers are correct, all columns and rows will add to the same number.

A. LIGHT
B. GREENSLEEVES
C. TILLERMAN
D. LOGAN
E. BOULDER
F. PEGGY
G. STEWART
H. NUN
I. WALLET
J. MASS
K. MENTAL
L. MONEY
M. MAYBETH
N. RETARDED
O. BOAT
P. GRANDMOTHER

1. Song Maybeth sang with Stewart
2. James stole money from him in the dormitory room.
3. Kind of hospital Dicey's mother is in, in Massachusetts
4. Word Fr. Joseph applies to Maybeth in his discussion with Dicey
5. Persuades Sammy to start walking to Bridgeport
6. Lou & Edie stole this from Edie's father.
7. Cousin Eunice must abandon her plans for becoming one.
8. James says the only true, unchanging thing is the speed of ___.
9. Dicey decides to go to Crisfield to meet her ___.
10. Dicey made Sammy return the ___ he stole that had $20 in it.
11. James fell off one at Rockland State Park.
12. Eunice's last name
13. Family name for Dicey & siblings
14. Character in a song the children's mother taught them: ___-O
15. Cousin Eunice goes to this every morning at 6:30.
16. Dicey found one in the barn.

A=8	B=1	C=13	D=12
E=11	F=14	G=2	H=7
I=10	J=15	K=3	L=6
M=5	N=4	O=16	P=9

Homecoming Word Search 1

Abigail Tillerman lives there. (9)
Character in a song the children's mother taught them: ___-O (5)
Cousin Eunice goes to this every morning at 6:30. (4)
Cousin Eunice must abandon her plans for becoming one. (3)
Dicey decides to go to Crisfield to meet her ___. (11)
Dicey figures the expense of staying with cousin Eunice is the cost of always being this. (8)
Dicey found one in the barn. (4)
Dicey got $57 for the sale of her mother's. (3)
Dicey got a job washing them. (7)
Dicey made Sammy return the ___ he stole that had $20 in it. (6)
Eunice told the children that Aunt Cilla had ___. (4)
Eunice's last name (5)
Family name for Dicey & siblings (9)
Father ___: Cousin Eunice's friend & spiritual counselor (6)
Grandmother said her husband used these to build a wall to keep things out. (5)
He always argues with Dicey's decisions. (5)
He chased the children with his dogs. (7)
He drove the children to Crisfield. (4)
James fell off one at Rockland State Park. (7)
James says the only true, unchanging thing is the speed of ___. (5)
James stole money from him in the dormitory room. (7)
Jerry allows Dicey to do ___ the boat. (5)
Kind of expression Dicey's grandmother's picture had (4)
Kind of hospital Dicey's mother is in, in Massachusetts (6)
Lou & Edie stole this from Edie's father. (5)
Persuades Sammy to start walking to Bridgeport (7)
Sammy caught them at Rockland State Park. (4)
She ran off Mr. Rudyard & rescued the children. (6)
Song Maybeth sang with Stewart (12)
The Tillerman children learn to eat these at their grandmother's house. (5)
The children ate at McDonalds and bought a ___ in Fairfield. (3)
The children ate mussels & clams at this state park. (8)
The children decide to make money by becoming ___ pickers. (6)
The children met Jerry & Tom at a boatyard there. (9)
The mall guard, Lou, & Edie believe Dicey is a boy named ___. (5)
The storekeeper in St. Michaels sounded like Dicey's ___. (6)
Where the children slept after rowing across the river (8)

Homecoming Word Search 1 Answer Key

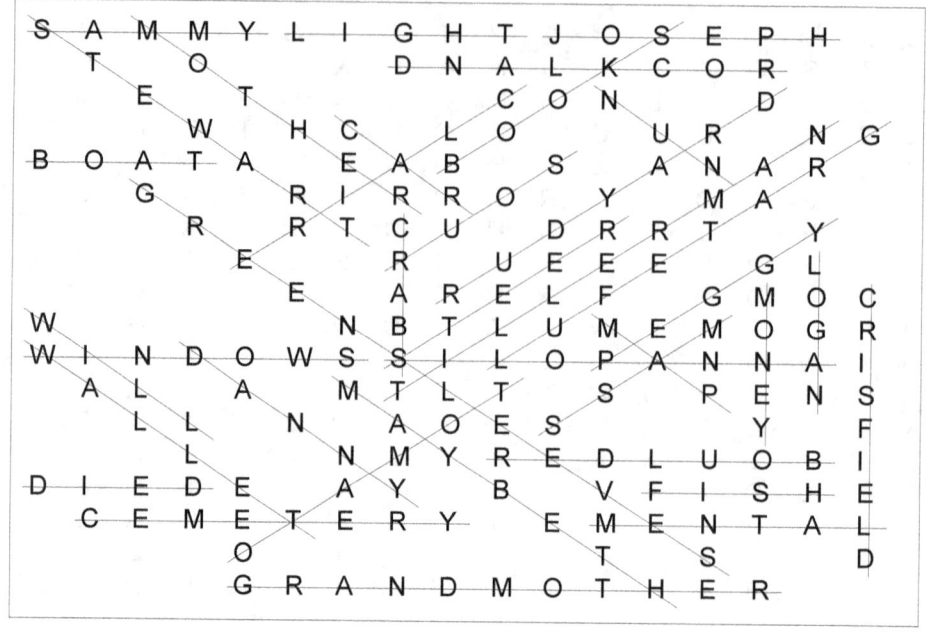

Abigail Tillerman lives there. (9)
Character in a song the children's mother taught them: ___-O (5)
Cousin Eunice goes to this every morning at 6:30. (4)
Cousin Eunice must abandon her plans for becoming one. (3)
Dicey decides to go to Crisfield to meet her ___. (11)
Dicey figures the expense of staying with cousin Eunice is the cost of always being this. (8)
Dicey found one in the barn. (4)
Dicey got $57 for the sale of her mother's. (3)
Dicey got a job washing them. (7)
Dicey made Sammy return the ___ he stole that had $20 in it. (6)
Eunice told the children that Aunt Cilla had ___. (4)
Eunice's last name (5)
Family name for Dicey & siblings (9)
Father ___: Cousin Eunice's friend & spiritual counselor (6)
Grandmother said her husband used these to build a wall to keep things out. (5)
He always argues with Dicey's decisions. (5)
He chased the children with his dogs. (7)
He drove the children to Crisfield. (4)
James fell off one at Rockland State Park. (7)
James says the only true, unchanging thing is the speed of ___. (5)

James stole money from him in the dormitory room. (7)
Jerry allows Dicey to do ___ the boat. (5)
Kind of expression Dicey's grandmother's picture had (4)
Kind of hospital Dicey's mother is in, in Massachusetts (6)
Lou & Edie stole this from Edie's father. (5)
Persuades Sammy to start walking to Bridgeport (7)
Sammy caught them at Rockland State Park. (4)
She ran off Mr. Rudyard & rescued the children. (6)
Song Maybeth sang with Stewart (12)
The Tillerman children learn to eat these at their grandmother's house. (5)
The children ate at McDonalds and bought a ___ in Fairfield. (3)
The children ate mussels & clams at this state park. (8)
The children decide to make money by becoming ___ pickers. (6)
The children met Jerry & Tom at a boatyard there. (9)
The mall guard, Lou, & Edie believe Dicey is a boy named ___. (5)
The storekeeper in St. Michaels sounded like Dicey's ___. (6)
Where the children slept after rowing across the river (8)

Homecoming Word Search 2

```
X B B O U L D E R W G H S S Z K S
R K R I S W O D N I W G T O L P T
L O A N C H T H H L Z W E U G K K
J Z C G T Y L W H L B H W R W S N
L W C K E C C D D H P Z A Y F H C
P N L N L J D L M P C N R R I M L
J M O E W A A E E M D W T E S A P
F M G R F K N T O M A T O T H P P
N J A I S T N D O L D Y H E S K T
U W N A A Y Y T L J E G B M J S V
N P G L X Z H E O L I N G E A V F
J E B C S E T S B L D T R C T S Z
B G G D R A E W D O R K A S C H S
V G S S E P M J S S A H T M R F M
V Y Q T H V Z M K N Y T E Q A H S
N R E E T S P O Y T D P F Q B F X
N W Z Y O X O L X N U R U S S F Q
T J F J M B C N A M R E L L I T B
```

Character in a song the children's mother taught them: ___-O (5)
Cousin Eunice goes to this every morning at 6:30. (4)
Cousin Eunice must abandon her plans for becoming one. (3)
Dicey decides to go to Crisfield to meet her ___. (11)
Dicey figures the expense of staying with cousin Eunice is the cost of always being this. (8)
Dicey found one in the barn. (4)
Dicey got $57 for the sale of her mother's. (3)
Dicey got a job washing them. (7)
Dicey made Sammy return the ___ he stole that had $20 in it. (6)
Each child received one when Will & Claire visited the farm. (7)
Eunice told the children that Aunt Cilla had ___. (4)
Eunice's last name (5)
Family name for Dicey & siblings (9)
Father ___: Cousin Eunice's friend & spiritual counselor (6)
Grandmother said her husband used these to build a wall to keep things out. (5)
He always argues with Dicey's decisions. (5)
He chased the children with his dogs. (7)
He drove the children to Crisfield. (4)
James fell off one at Rockland State Park. (7)
James says the only true, unchanging thing is the speed of ___. (5)
James stole money from him in the dormitory room. (7)
Jerry allows Dicey to do ___ the boat. (5)
Kind of expression Dicey's grandmother's picture had (4)
Kind of hospital Dicey's mother is in, in Massachusetts (6)
Lou & Edie stole this from Edie's father. (5)
Persuades Sammy to start walking to Bridgeport (7)
Sammy caught them at Rockland State Park. (4)
She ran off Mr. Rudyard & rescued the children. (6)
The Tillerman children learn to eat these at their grandmother's house. (5)
The children ate at McDonalds and bought a ___ in Fairfield. (3)
The children ate mussels & clams at this state park. (8)
The children decide to make money by becoming ___ pickers. (6)
The mall guard, Lou, & Edie believe Dicey is a boy named ___. (5)
The storekeeper in St. Michaels sounded like Dicey's ___. (6)
Where the children slept after rowing across the river (8)

Homecoming Word Search 2 Answer Key

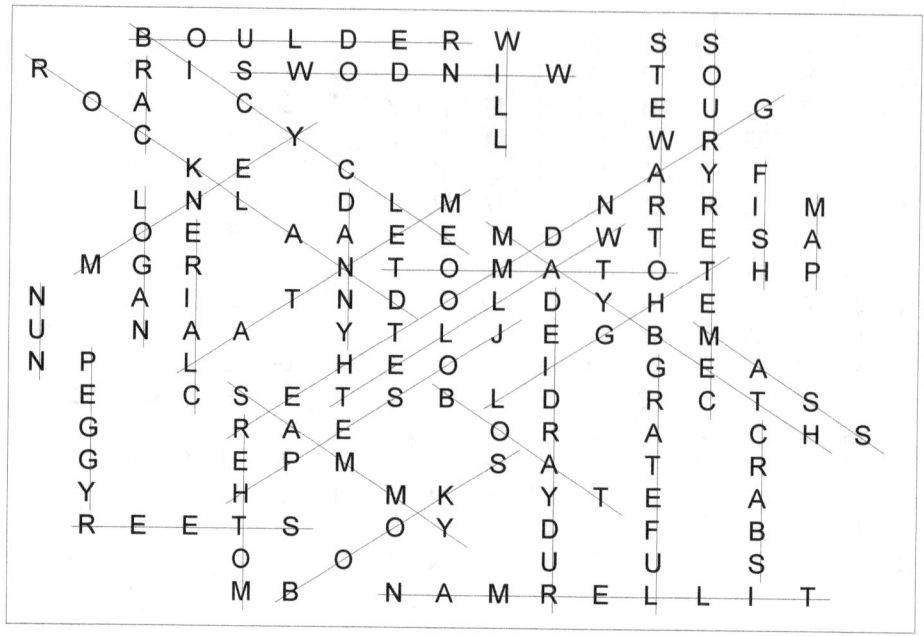

Character in a song the children's mother taught them: ___-O (5)
Cousin Eunice goes to this every morning at 6:30. (4)
Cousin Eunice must abandon her plans for becoming one. (3)
Dicey decides to go to Crisfield to meet her ___. (11)
Dicey figures the expense of staying with cousin Eunice is the cost of always being this. (8)
Dicey found one in the barn. (4)
Dicey got $57 for the sale of her mother's. (3)
Dicey got a job washing them. (7)
Dicey made Sammy return the ___ he stole that had $20 in it. (6)
Each child received one when Will & Claire visited the farm. (7)
Eunice told the children that Aunt Cilla had ___. (4)
Eunice's last name (5)
Family name for Dicey & siblings (9)
Father ___: Cousin Eunice's friend & spiritual counselor (6)
Grandmother said her husband used these to build a wall to keep things out. (5)
He always argues with Dicey's decisions. (5)
He chased the children with his dogs. (7)
He drove the children to Crisfield. (4)
James fell off one at Rockland State Park. (7)
James says the only true, unchanging thing is the speed of ___. (5)
James stole money from him in the dormitory room. (7)
Jerry allows Dicey to do ___ the boat. (5)
Kind of expression Dicey's grandmother's picture had (4)
Kind of hospital Dicey's mother is in, in Massachusetts (6)
Lou & Edie stole this from Edie's father. (5)
Persuades Sammy to start walking to Bridgeport (7)
Sammy caught them at Rockland State Park. (4)
She ran off Mr. Rudyard & rescued the children. (6)
The Tillerman children learn to eat these at their grandmother's house. (5)
The children ate at McDonalds and bought a ___ in Fairfield. (3)
The children ate mussels & clams at this state park. (8)
The children decide to make money by becoming ___ pickers. (6)
The mall guard, Lou, & Edie believe Dicey is a boy named ___. (5)
The storekeeper in St. Michaels sounded like Dicey's ___. (6)
Where the children slept after rowing across the river (8)

Homecoming Word Search 3

```
F Y C P W V E R R I C K E R D I E D L
I P R F W I E F S V G F B E E Q W Y L M
S B A L J T L D C A N H H B D K I W W H
H S B N A G O L C G M T D R L Y N N A D
R B S R X P Q X R A O M G I U Z D K M G
J P D R S P X K Y M T C Y D O Z O B O M
P E U G G W C B D P H E A G B D W Q N K
D O G H Q R E N Q E E M N E L O S B E J
S C R X T T A Q K G R E N P T I O H Y J
B B E G H R Q T R G J T A O S A G K V T
M P E V G L W R E Y T E P R T T R H S R
M T N J C F B A L F X R O T Q J S D T H
G C S R H V N K L N U Y L C R G B H K S
C B L O T P A X K L G L I S V S X Y V R
Y P E C M G M M F B E Y S L Z T G S U C
F W E K E D R H T W M T S F L E H D L T
O P V L N N E P S M Q H J X L W Y A Q S
T Z E A T B L L T Q Y P T X C Z A I R Q
A P S N A B L K J E V R Y G R R N E M R
M K B D L E I F S I R C Q D E T E Y A Z
O A M Z C F T O J Z I W A B V T B Z S R
T G P M Q G J C K B N U N R S M Z D S L
```

ANNAPOLIS	CRABS	LIGHT	PEGGY	TOMATO
BICYCLE	CRISFIELD	LOGAN	RETARDED	VERRICKER
BOAT	DANNY	MAP	ROCKLAND	WALLET
BOOKS	DIED	MASS	RUDYARD	WILL
BOULDER	FISH	MAYBETH	SAMMY	WINDOWS
BRIDGEPORT	GRANDMOTHER	MENTAL	SOUR	
CAR	GRATEFUL	MONEY	STEER	
CEMETERY	GREENSLEEVES	MOTHER	STEWART	
CLAIRE	JOSEPH	NUN	TILLERMAN	

Homecoming Word Search 3 Answer Key

ANNAPOLIS	CRABS	LIGHT	PEGGY	TOMATO
BICYCLE	CRISFIELD	LOGAN	RETARDED	VERRICKER
BOAT	DANNY	MAP	ROCKLAND	WALLET
BOOKS	DIED	MASS	RUDYARD	WILL
BOULDER	FISH	MAYBETH	SAMMY	WINDOWS
BRIDGEPORT	GRANDMOTHER	MENTAL	SOUR	
CAR	GRATEFUL	MONEY	STEER	
CEMETERY	GREENSLEEVES	MOTHER	STEWART	
CLAIRE	JOSEPH	NUN	TILLERMAN	

Homecoming Word Search 4

```
C B I C Y C L E R E T A R D E D X K R D
E G R A N D M O T H E R M T N Y L M T F Y
M S B N G X D T D S M F C A Y G O L H P
E R V E R I C K E R P L B P E G G Y A S
T J Z M S Q P X Y S N K J T S F P C L H
E W T Q Y R Y G G C C L D P I X D C N G
R P H Y H X S M O F L B W L D V R N V
Y H S W S F K T R Q E S O I O H B D W X
M G C L T B F X I I N W U N P K X X Y W
M G R N P H D P F L L T L D A L R Q Z Q
X W A T P F S S H W L Z D O N I T Z Z
M S B E B P Q R V C E E W N X O G D R
S M S O U R E H T O M W R S A M Y H T
M O T T C X I F G A O I A M L N W J H
J H A R E K S D S N N L C T A N L Q M J
S O B N R W M S G H E L O B A N R E H L
B M R U D Y A R D E Y F M D O M A P T C
V D D N Y L Y R Y S P S I E N O V L E N
J Z P I J T N K T M P O Q S N J K D B K
G R A T E F U L C L A I R E H T F S Y Z
H F D L P D N C S P N J M T S H A B A K
G R E E N S L E E V E S T E E R K L M
```

ANNAPOLIS   CRABS   LIGHT   PEGGY   TOMATO

BICYCLE   CRISFIELD   LOGAN   RETARDED   VERRICKER

BOAT   DANNY   MAP   ROCKLAND   WALLET

BOOKS   DIED   MASS   RUDYARD   WILL

BOULDER   FISH   MAYBETH   SAMMY   WINDOWS

BRIDGEPORT   GRANDMOTHER   MENTAL   SOUR

CAR   GRATEFUL   MONEY   STEER

CEMETERY   GREENSLEEVES MOTHER   STEWART

CLAIRE   JOSEPH   NUN   TILLERMAN

Homecoming Word Search 4 Answer Key

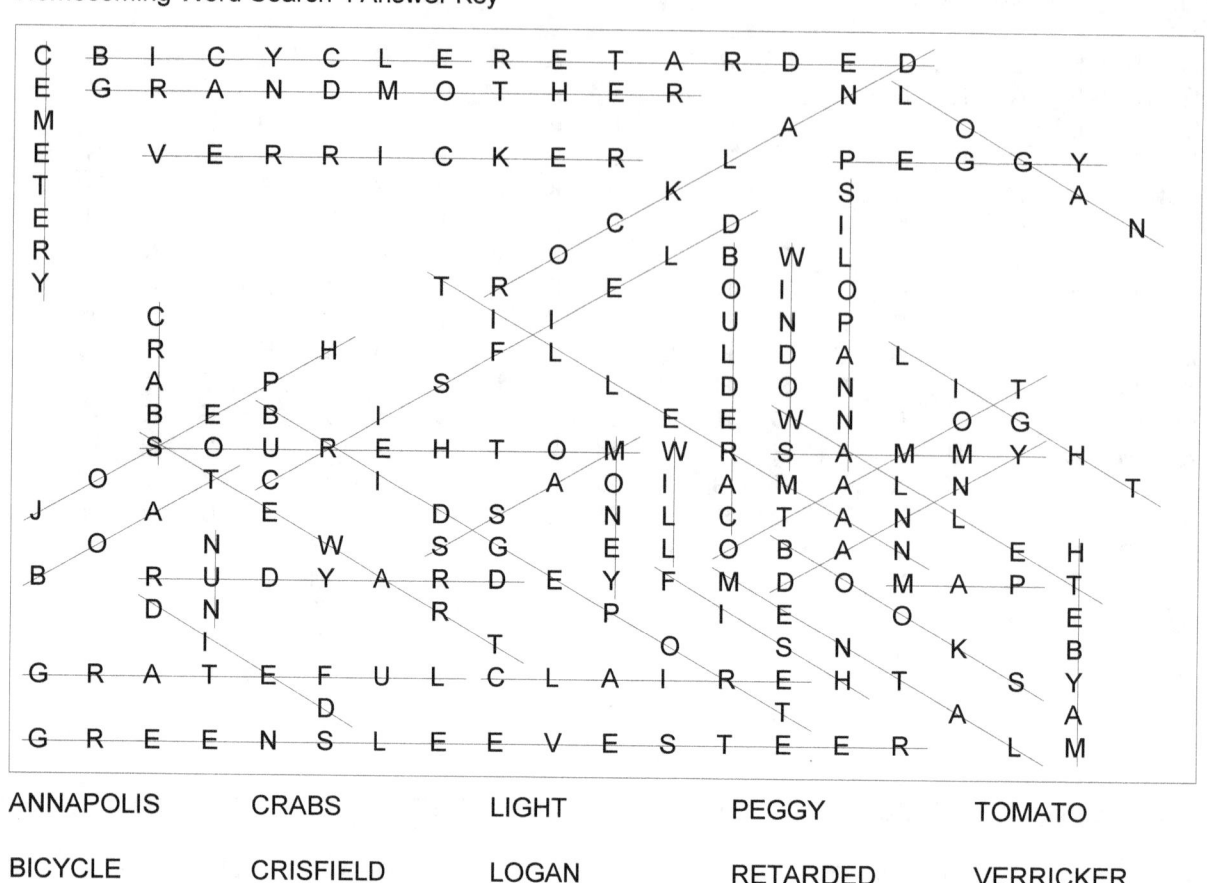

ANNAPOLIS	CRABS	LIGHT	PEGGY	TOMATO
BICYCLE	CRISFIELD	LOGAN	RETARDED	VERRICKER
BOAT	DANNY	MAP	ROCKLAND	WALLET
BOOKS	DIED	MASS	RUDYARD	WILL
BOULDER	FISH	MAYBETH	SAMMY	WINDOWS
BRIDGEPORT	GRANDMOTHER	MENTAL	SOUR	
CAR	GRATEFUL	MONEY	STEER	
CEMETERY	GREENSLEEVES	MOTHER	STEWART	
CLAIRE	JOSEPH	NUN	TILLERMAN	

Homecoming Crossword 1

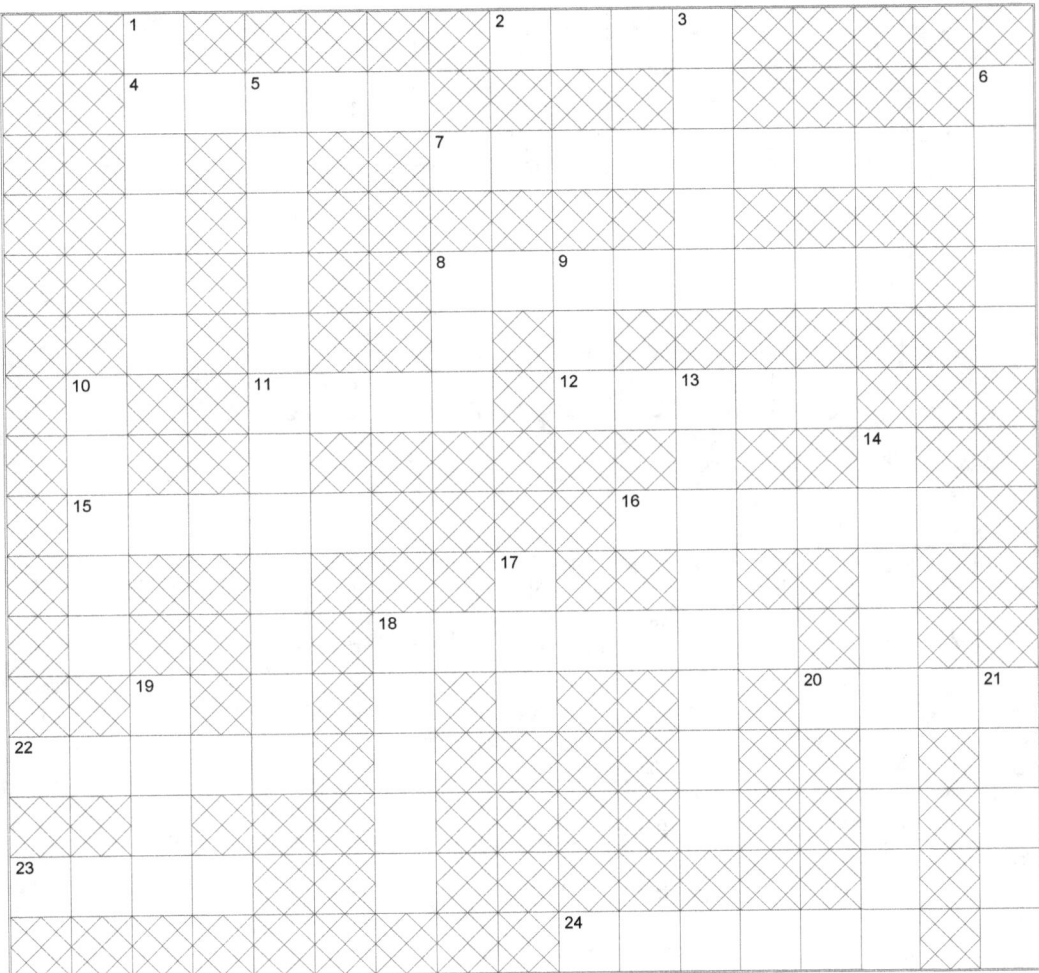

Across

2. He drove the children to Crisfield.
4. Eunice's last name
7. City where Aunt Cilla lived
8. Where the children slept after rowing across the river
11. Kind of expression Dicey's grandmother's picture had
12. Character in a song the children's mother taught them: ___-O
15. Lou & Edie stole this from Edie's father.
16. Dicey made Sammy return the ___ he stole that had $20 in it.
18. James fell off one at Rockland State Park.
20. Eunice told the children that Aunt Cilla had ___.
22. The Tillerman children learn to eat these at their grandmother's house.
23. Sammy caught them at Rockland State Park.
24. The storekeeper in St. Michaels sounded like Dicey's ___.

Down

1. She ran off Mr. Rudyard & rescued the children.
3. James says the only true, unchanging thing is the speed of ___.
5. Song Maybeth sang with Stewart
6. Jerry allows Dicey to do ___ the boat.
8. Dicey got $57 for the sale of her mother's.
9. The children ate at McDonalds and bought a ___ in Fairfield.
10. He always argues with Dicey's decisions.
13. Dicey figures the expense of staying with cousin Eunice is the cost of always being this.
14. Dicey's long-missing father's name: Francis ___
17. Cousin Eunice must abandon her plans for becoming one.
18. Grandmother said her husband used these to build a wall to keep things out.
19. Cousin Eunice goes to this every morning at 6:30.
21. The mall guard, Lou, & Edie believe Dicey is a boy named ___.

Homecoming Crossword 1 Answer Key

	1 C				2 W	I	3 L	L		
4 L	O	5 G	A	N			I			6 S
	A	R			7 B	R	I	D	G	E	P	O	R	T
	I	E					H			E
	R	E		8 C	9 M	E	T	E	R	Y	E
	E	N		A	A					R
10 S		11 S	O	U	R	12 P	E	13 G	G	Y
A		L				R		14 V
15 M	O	N	E	Y		16 W	A	L	L	E	T
M		E		17 N		T		R
Y		V		18 B	O	U	L	D	E	R	R
	19 M	E		O	N		F		20 D	I	E	21 D
22 C	R	A	B	S	O		U		C		A
	S			K		L		K		N
23 F	I	S	H		S				E		N
				24 M	O	T	H	E	R		Y

Across
2. He drove the children to Crisfield.
4. Eunice's last name
7. City where Aunt Cilla lived
8. Where the children slept after rowing across the river
11. Kind of expression Dicey's grandmother's picture had
12. Character in a song the children's mother taught them: ___-O
15. Lou & Edie stole this from Edie's father.
16. Dicey made Sammy return the ___ he stole that had $20 in it.
18. James fell off one at Rockland State Park.
20. Eunice told the children that Aunt Cilla had ___.
22. The Tillerman children learn to eat these at their grandmother's house.
23. Sammy caught them at Rockland State Park.
24. The storekeeper in St. Michaels sounded like Dicey's ___.

Down
1. She ran off Mr. Rudyard & rescued the children.
3. James says the only true, unchanging thing is the speed of ___.
5. Song Maybeth sang with Stewart
6. Jerry allows Dicey to do ___ the boat.
8. Dicey got $57 for the sale of her mother's.
9. The children ate at McDonalds and bought a ___ in Fairfield.
10. He always argues with Dicey's decisions.
13. Dicey figures the expense of staying with cousin Eunice is the cost of always being this.
14. Dicey's long-missing father's name: Francis ___
17. Cousin Eunice must abandon her plans for becoming one.
18. Grandmother said her husband used these to build a wall to keep things out.
19. Cousin Eunice goes to this every morning at 6:30.
21. The mall guard, Lou, & Edie believe Dicey is a boy named ___.

Homecoming Crossword 2

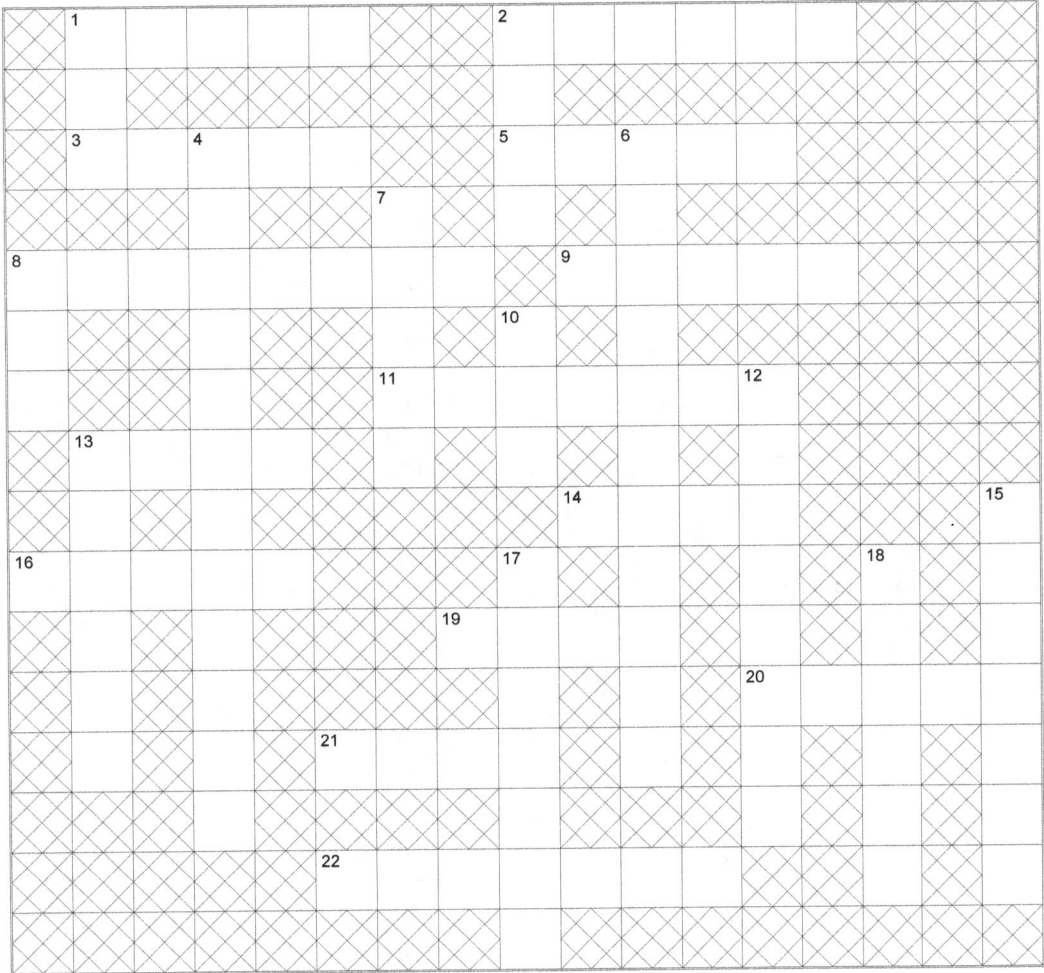

Across
1. Lou & Edie stole this from Edie's father.
2. Dicey made Sammy return the ___ he stole that had $20 in it.
3. Character in a song the children's mother taught them: ___-O
5. James says the only true, unchanging thing is the speed of ___.
8. Where the children slept after rowing across the river
9. He always argues with Dicey's decisions.
11. James fell off one at Rockland State Park.
13. Cousin Eunice goes to this every morning at 6:30.
14. Dicey found one in the barn.
16. Jerry allows Dicey to do ___ the boat.
19. Sammy caught them at Rockland State Park.
20. The mall guard, Lou, & Edie believe Dicey is a boy named ____.
21. Eunice told the children that Aunt Cilla had ___.
22. James stole money from him in the dormitory room.

Down
1. The children ate at McDonalds and bought a ___ in Fairfield.
2. He drove the children to Crisfield.
4. Song Maybeth sang with Stewart
6. Dicey decides to go to Crisfield to meet her ___.
7. The Tillerman children learn to eat these at their grandmother's house.
8. Dicey got $57 for the sale of her mother's.
10. Cousin Eunice must abandon her plans for becoming one.
12. Word Fr. Joseph applies to Maybeth in his discussion with Dicey
13. The storekeeper in St. Michaels sounded like Dicey's ___.
15. Each child received one when Will & Claire visited the farm.
17. Dicey got a job washing them.
18. Kind of hospital Dicey's mother is in, in Massachusetts

Homecoming Crossword 2 Answer Key

		1						2						
		M	O	N	E	Y		W	A	L	L	E	T	
		A						I						
		3		4				5		6				
		P	E	G	G	Y		L	I	G	H	T		
				R			7	L		R				
8							C							
C	E	M	E	T	E	R	Y		9	S	A	M	M	Y
A				E				10		N				
							A	N						
R				N		11				12				
						B	O	U	L	D	E	R		
		13												
		M	A	S	S		S		N		M			
		O		L				14			E		15	
								B	O	A	T		B	
16							17					18		
S	T	E	E	R			W		T		A	M		I
		H		E		19					R	E		C
						F	I	S	H					
		E		V				N		E	20	D	A	N	N	Y
						21								
		R		E		D	I	E	D		R	E		T		C
				S				O			D		A		L
				22										
				S	T	E	W	A	R	T		L		E
							S							

Across
1. Lou & Edie stole this from Edie's father.
2. Dicey made Sammy return the ___ he stole that had $20 in it.
3. Character in a song the children's mother taught them: ___-O
5. James says the only true, unchanging thing is the speed of ___.
8. Where the children slept after rowing across the river
9. He always argues with Dicey's decisions.
11. James fell off one at Rockland State Park.
13. Cousin Eunice goes to this every morning at 6:30.
14. Dicey found one in the barn.
16. Jerry allows Dicey to do ___ the boat.
19. Sammy caught them at Rockland State Park.
20. The mall guard, Lou, & Edie believe Dicey is a boy named ____.
21. Eunice told the children that Aunt Cilla had ___.
22. James stole money from him in the dormitory room.

Down
1. The children ate at McDonalds and bought a ___ in Fairfield.
2. He drove the children to Crisfield.
4. Song Maybeth sang with Stewart
6. Dicey decides to go to Crisfield to meet her ___.
7. The Tillerman children learn to eat these at their grandmother's house.
8. Dicey got $57 for the sale of her mother's.
10. Cousin Eunice must abandon her plans for becoming one.
12. Word Fr. Joseph applies to Maybeth in his discussion with Dicey
13. The storekeeper in St. Michaels sounded like Dicey's ___.
15. Each child received one when Will & Claire visited the farm.
17. Dicey got a job washing them.
18. Kind of hospital Dicey's mother is in, in Massachusetts

Homecoming Crossword 3

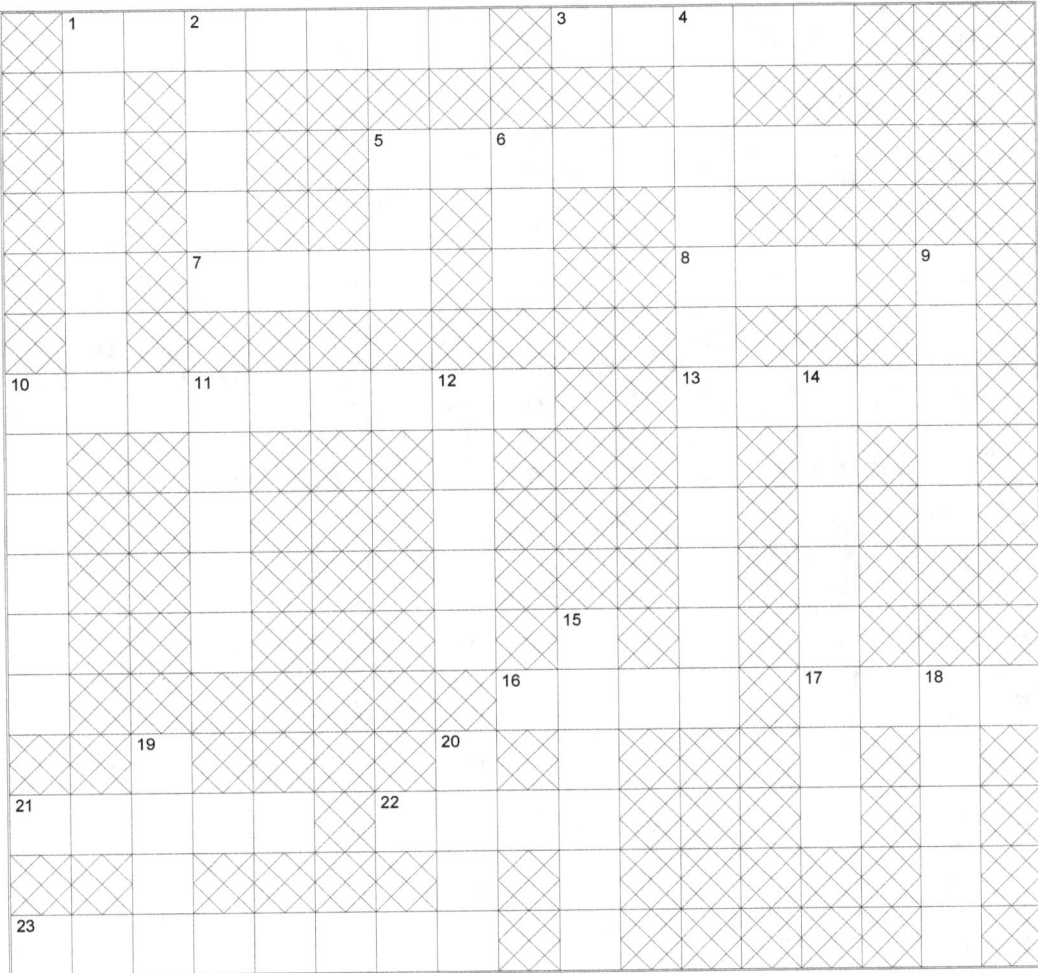

Across
1. Each child received one when Will & Claire visited the farm.
3. Character in a song the children's mother taught them: ___-O
5. Where the children slept after rowing across the river
7. Kind of expression Dicey's grandmother's picture had
8. Cousin Eunice must abandon her plans for becoming one.
10. Abigail Tillerman lives there.
13. Eunice's last name
16. Cousin Eunice goes to this every morning at 6:30.
17. Sammy caught them at Rockland State Park.
21. Grandmother said her husband used these to build a wall to keep things out.
22. He drove the children to Crisfield.
23. Word Fr. Joseph applies to Maybeth in his discussion with Dicey

Down
1. James fell off one at Rockland State Park.
2. The Tillerman children learn to eat these at their grandmother's house.
4. Song Maybeth sang with Stewart
5. Dicey got $57 for the sale of her mother's.
6. The children ate at McDonalds and bought a __ in Fairfield.
9. Lou & Edie stole this from Edie's father.
10. She ran off Mr. Rudyard & rescued the children.
11. He always argues with Dicey's decisions.
12. James says the only true, unchanging thing is the speed of ___.
14. Dicey figures the expense of staying with cousin Eunice is the cost of always being this.
15. Dicey made Sammy return the ___ he stole that had $20 in it.
18. Jerry allows Dicey to do ___ the boat.
19. Dicey found one in the barn.
20. Eunice told the children that Aunt Cilla had ___.

41
Copyrighted

Homecoming Crossword 3 Answer Key

	1	2					3	4		
	B	I	C	Y	C	L	E	P	E	G	G	Y
	O		R					R		
	U		A		5		6			
					C	E	M	E	T	E	R	Y
	L		B		A		A			
	7							8		9
	D	S	O	U	R		P	N	U	N	M
	E							S		O
10		11			12			13		14
C	R	I	S	F	I	E	L	D	L	O	G	A	N
L		A			I			E		R	E
A		M			G			E		A	Y
I		M			H			V		T
R		Y			T		15	E		E
E							W			
						16			17		18
						M	A	S	S	F	I	S	H
		19				20				
		B				D		L		U	T
21					22					
B	O	O	K	S	W	I	L	L		L	E
		A				E		E			E
23										
R	E	T	A	R	D	E	D	T			R

Across
1. Each child received one when Will & Claire visited the farm.
3. Character in a song the children's mother taught them: ___-O
5. Where the children slept after rowing across the river
7. Kind of expression Dicey's grandmother's picture had
8. Cousin Eunice must abandon her plans for becoming one.
10. Abigail Tillerman lives there.
13. Eunice's last name
16. Cousin Eunice goes to this every morning at 6:30.
17. Sammy caught them at Rockland State Park.
21. Grandmother said her husband used these to build a wall to keep things out.
22. He drove the children to Crisfield.
23. Word Fr. Joseph applies to Maybeth in his discussion with Dicey

Down
1. James fell off one at Rockland State Park.
2. The Tillerman children learn to eat these at their grandmother's house.
4. Song Maybeth sang with Stewart
5. Dicey got $57 for the sale of her mother's.
6. The children ate at McDonalds and bought a __ in Fairfield.
9. Lou & Edie stole this from Edie's father.
10. She ran off Mr. Rudyard & rescued the children.
11. He always argues with Dicey's decisions.
12. James says the only true, unchanging thing is the speed of ___.
14. Dicey figures the expense of staying with cousin Eunice is the cost of always being this.
15. Dicey made Sammy return the ___ he stole that had $20 in it.
18. Jerry allows Dicey to do ___ the boat.
19. Dicey found one in the barn.
20. Eunice told the children that Aunt Cilla had ___.

Homecoming Crossword 4

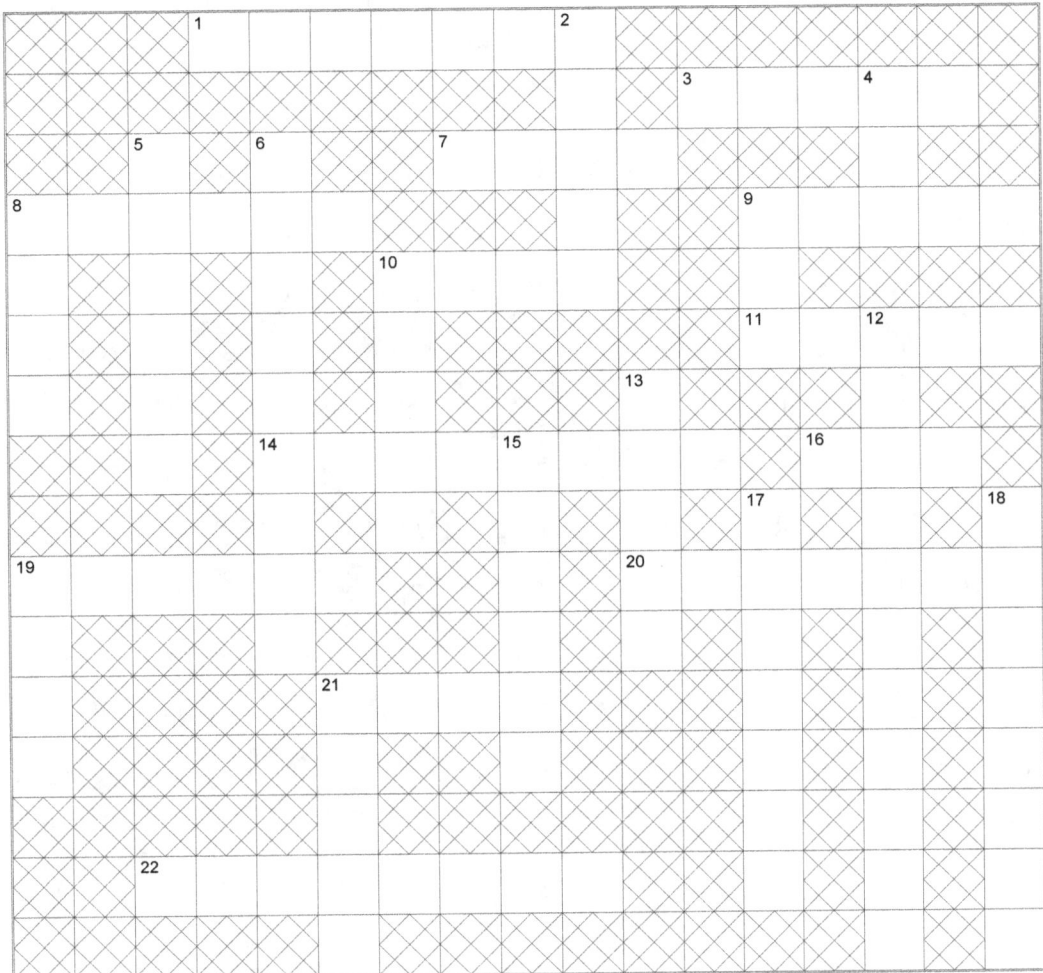

Across
1. Dicey got a job washing them.
3. The mall guard, Lou, & Edie believe Dicey is a boy named ___.
7. Eunice told the children that Aunt Cilla had ___.
8. Dicey made Sammy return the ___ he stole that had $20 in it.
9. Lou & Edie stole this from Edie's father.
10. Kind of expression Dicey's grandmother's picture had
11. Character in a song the children's mother taught them: ___-O
14. Where the children slept after rowing across the river
16. Dicey got $57 for the sale of her mother's.
19. The storekeeper in St. Michaels sounded like Dicey's ___.
20. James fell off one at Rockland State Park.
21. Dicey found one in the barn.
22. The children ate mussels & clams at this state park.

Down
2. Jerry allows Dicey to do ___ the boat.
4. Cousin Eunice must abandon her plans for becoming one.
5. She ran off Mr. Rudyard & rescued the children.
6. Dicey's long-missing father's name: Francis ___
8. He drove the children to Crisfield.
9. The children ate at McDonalds and bought a ___ in Fairfield.
10. He always argues with Dicey's decisions.
12. Dicey decides to go to Crisfield to meet her ___.
13. The Tillerman children learn to eat these at their grandmother's house.
15. The children decide to make money by becoming ___ pickers.
17. He chased the children with his dogs.
18. Dicey figures the expense of staying with cousin Eunice is the cost of always being this.
19. Cousin Eunice goes to this every morning at 6:30.
21. Grandmother said her husband used these to build a wall to keep things out.

Homecoming Crossword 4 Answer Key

				1 W	I	N	D	O	W	2 S					
										T		3 D	A	N	N	4 Y
		5 C		6 V		7 D	I	E	D						U
8 W	A	L	L	E	T				E			9 M	O	N	E	Y
I		A		R			10 S	O	U	R		A			
L		I		R			A				11 P	E	12 G	G	Y
L		R		I			M			13 C			R		
		E		14 C	E	M	E	15 T	E	R	Y		16 C	A	R
				K			Y		O		A		17 R	N	18 G
19 M	O	T	H	E	R				M		20 B	O	U	L	D	E	R
A				R					A		S		D		M		A
S				21 B	O	A	T					Y		O		T
S				O							A		T		E
				O							R		H		F
		22 R	O	C	K	L	A	N	D		D		E		U
				S									R		L

Across
1. Dicey got a job washing them.
3. The mall guard, Lou, & Edie believe Dicey is a boy named ___.
7. Eunice told the children that Aunt Cilla had ___.
8. Dicey made Sammy return the ___ he stole that had $20 in it.
9. Lou & Edie stole this from Edie's father.
10. Kind of expression Dicey's grandmother's picture had
11. Character in a song the children's mother taught them: ___-O
14. Where the children slept after rowing across the river
16. Dicey got $57 for the sale of her mother's.
19. The storekeeper in St. Michaels sounded like Dicey's ___.
20. James fell off one at Rockland State Park.
21. Dicey found one in the barn.
22. The children ate mussels & clams at this state park.

Down
2. Jerry allows Dicey to do ___ the boat.
4. Cousin Eunice must abandon her plans for becoming one.
5. She ran off Mr. Rudyard & rescued the children.
6. Dicey's long-missing father's name: Francis ___
8. He drove the children to Crisfield.
9. The children ate at McDonalds and bought a ___ in Fairfield.
10. He always argues with Dicey's decisions.
12. Dicey decides to go to Crisfield to meet her ___.
13. The Tillerman children learn to eat these at their grandmother's house.
15. The children decide to make money by becoming ___ pickers.
17. He chased the children with his dogs.
18. Dicey figures the expense of staying with cousin Eunice is the cost of always being this.
19. Cousin Eunice goes to this every morning at 6:30.
21. Grandmother said her husband used these to build a wall to keep things out.

Homecoming

PEGGY	LOGAN	TOMATO	CAR	BOOKS
STEER	RUDYARD	RETARDED	CLAIRE	VERRICKER
GRATEFUL	STEWART	FREE SPACE	MONEY	MENTAL
WALLET	MAP	JOSEPH	TILLERMAN	WINDOWS
ANNAPOLIS	SAMMY	DIED	SOUR	MAYBETH

Homecoming

FISH	BOULDER	BRIDGEPORT	CRABS	GRANDMOTHER
BICYCLE	MASS	CRISFIELD	NUN	CEMETERY
GREENSLEEVES	BOAT	FREE SPACE	LIGHT	DANNY
WILL	MAYBETH	SOUR	DIED	SAMMY
ANNAPOLIS	WINDOWS	TILLERMAN	JOSEPH	MAP

Homecoming

MONEY	MOTHER	BRIDGEPORT	TILLERMAN	CRISFIELD
GRATEFUL	CAR	RUDYARD	RETARDED	BICYCLE
SAMMY	JOSEPH	FREE SPACE	GRANDMOTHER	FISH
STEER	WALLET	WILL	ROCKLAND	MAP
BOAT	STEWART	DIED	MAYBETH	DANNY

Homecoming

LIGHT	CLAIRE	TOMATO	PEGGY	BOULDER
BOOKS	GREENSLEEVES	WINDOWS	CRABS	SOUR
NUN	MASS	FREE SPACE	ANNAPOLIS	LOGAN
VERRICKER	DANNY	MAYBETH	DIED	STEWART
BOAT	MAP	ROCKLAND	WILL	WALLET

Homecoming

CLAIRE	BOAT	FISH	STEER	CEMETERY
WILL	TOMATO	BOULDER	MASS	SOUR
MAP	BRIDGEPORT	FREE SPACE	WALLET	BOOKS
WINDOWS	DANNY	GREENSLEEVES	ANNAPOLIS	CRABS
TILLERMAN	MAYBETH	STEWART	VERRICKER	JOSEPH

Homecoming

GRANDMOTHER	ROCKLAND	MOTHER	GRATEFUL	LIGHT
RUDYARD	DIED	MONEY	MENTAL	NUN
CAR	SAMMY	FREE SPACE	LOGAN	BICYCLE
RETARDED	JOSEPH	VERRICKER	STEWART	MAYBETH
TILLERMAN	CRABS	ANNAPOLIS	GREENSLEEVES	DANNY

Homecoming

SOUR	CRISFIELD	ROCKLAND	GREENSLEEVES	TOMATO
BOOKS	MOTHER	WILL	MENTAL	RETARDED
CEMETERY	MAP	FREE SPACE	MAYBETH	DANNY
RUDYARD	CLAIRE	MASS	PEGGY	ANNAPOLIS
WINDOWS	STEER	BOULDER	BICYCLE	STEWART

Homecoming

DIED	VERRICKER	FISH	CAR	BOAT
JOSEPH	MONEY	SAMMY	NUN	TILLERMAN
CRABS	BRIDGEPORT	FREE SPACE	GRANDMOTHER	WALLET
LOGAN	STEWART	BICYCLE	BOULDER	STEER
WINDOWS	ANNAPOLIS	PEGGY	MASS	CLAIRE

Homecoming

CRABS	TOMATO	MOTHER	GRANDMOTHER	STEER
ANNAPOLIS	CEMETERY	VERRICKER	DIED	SAMMY
GREENSLEEVES	STEWART	FREE SPACE	BICYCLE	LOGAN
WALLET	CRISFIELD	MAP	PEGGY	MENTAL
MAYBETH	WINDOWS	FISH	CAR	BOOKS

Homecoming

TILLERMAN	GRATEFUL	CLAIRE	RETARDED	NUN
BOULDER	MASS	LIGHT	JOSEPH	BRIDGEPORT
WILL	ROCKLAND	FREE SPACE	MONEY	RUDYARD
BOAT	BOOKS	CAR	FISH	WINDOWS
MAYBETH	MENTAL	PEGGY	MAP	CRISFIELD

Homecoming

WILL	SOUR	BICYCLE	PEGGY	CRISFIELD
WALLET	MENTAL	MONEY	DIED	CEMETERY
BOULDER	LIGHT	FREE SPACE	NUN	WINDOWS
LOGAN	ROCKLAND	RUDYARD	RETARDED	SAMMY
MASS	STEER	VERRICKER	CAR	BRIDGEPORT

Homecoming

ANNAPOLIS	GREENSLEEVES	TOMATO	MAP	MAYBETH
BOAT	STEWART	CRABS	DANNY	GRANDMOTHER
CLAIRE	MOTHER	FREE SPACE	FISH	GRATEFUL
BOOKS	BRIDGEPORT	CAR	VERRICKER	STEER
MASS	SAMMY	RETARDED	RUDYARD	ROCKLAND

Homecoming

WALLET	ANNAPOLIS	CRABS	MAP	BICYCLE
TOMATO	CAR	MAYBETH	GREENSLEEVES	WINDOWS
WILL	DIED	FREE SPACE	GRANDMOTHER	CEMETERY
BOULDER	STEWART	MASS	NUN	VERRICKER
BOOKS	STEER	TILLERMAN	SOUR	RETARDED

Homecoming

BOAT	JOSEPH	MOTHER	MENTAL	PEGGY
FISH	ROCKLAND	CRISFIELD	DANNY	LIGHT
BRIDGEPORT	CLAIRE	FREE SPACE	SAMMY	LOGAN
RUDYARD	RETARDED	SOUR	TILLERMAN	STEER
BOOKS	VERRICKER	NUN	MASS	STEWART

51
Copyrighted

Homecoming

LIGHT	DIED	CAR	BOAT	WILL
TOMATO	BOULDER	SOUR	WALLET	MASS
STEWART	MAP	FREE SPACE	RUDYARD	ANNAPOLIS
DANNY	MENTAL	GRATEFUL	FISH	GRANDMOTHER
LOGAN	STEER	CRISFIELD	VERRICKER	BICYCLE

Homecoming

RETARDED	TILLERMAN	PEGGY	CLAIRE	NUN
BOOKS	MONEY	JOSEPH	MAYBETH	CRABS
MOTHER	CEMETERY	FREE SPACE	BRIDGEPORT	GREENSLEEVES
ROCKLAND	BICYCLE	VERRICKER	CRISFIELD	STEER
LOGAN	GRANDMOTHER	FISH	GRATEFUL	MENTAL

Homecoming

WILL	MOTHER	MENTAL	CEMETERY	CRABS
WALLET	MASS	RETARDED	SOUR	ANNAPOLIS
RUDYARD	TILLERMAN	FREE SPACE	PEGGY	CLAIRE
GREENSLEEVES	DANNY	MONEY	STEER	GRATEFUL
SAMMY	BOOKS	DIED	BOULDER	MAYBETH

Homecoming

STEWART	GRANDMOTHER	LOGAN	BICYCLE	CAR
BOAT	MAP	TOMATO	NUN	ROCKLAND
FISH	CRISFIELD	FREE SPACE	BRIDGEPORT	LIGHT
WINDOWS	MAYBETH	BOULDER	DIED	BOOKS
SAMMY	GRATEFUL	STEER	MONEY	DANNY

Homecoming

DANNY	DIED	BOAT	CRISFIELD	MOTHER
MENTAL	GREENSLEEVES	VERRICKER	BRIDGEPORT	CRABS
LIGHT	LOGAN	FREE SPACE	GRANDMOTHER	NUN
SAMMY	WILL	WINDOWS	BICYCLE	SOUR
ROCKLAND	TILLERMAN	PEGGY	FISH	MAYBETH

Homecoming

MAP	ANNAPOLIS	CLAIRE	CAR	TOMATO
MASS	BOOKS	CEMETERY	JOSEPH	STEWART
RUDYARD	BOULDER	FREE SPACE	RETARDED	GRATEFUL
STEER	MAYBETH	FISH	PEGGY	TILLERMAN
ROCKLAND	SOUR	BICYCLE	WINDOWS	WILL

Homecoming

MASS	STEER	BICYCLE	MOTHER	TILLERMAN
SOUR	BRIDGEPORT	BOULDER	RUDYARD	MONEY
RETARDED	STEWART	FREE SPACE	JOSEPH	GRATEFUL
GRANDMOTHER	WILL	LOGAN	CRABS	WALLET
BOAT	VERRICKER	CRISFIELD	CLAIRE	TOMATO

Homecoming

MENTAL	PEGGY	DIED	LIGHT	DANNY
NUN	WINDOWS	CAR	MAP	FISH
GREENSLEEVES	BOOKS	FREE SPACE	MAYBETH	ROCKLAND
CEMETERY	TOMATO	CLAIRE	CRISFIELD	VERRICKER
BOAT	WALLET	CRABS	LOGAN	WILL

Homecoming

VERRICKER	DANNY	LOGAN	TILLERMAN	SAMMY
FISH	WILL	GREENSLEEVES	ROCKLAND	MONEY
BOOKS	PEGGY	FREE SPACE	NUN	MENTAL
RUDYARD	GRANDMOTHER	LIGHT	JOSEPH	MASS
ANNAPOLIS	CAR	CRISFIELD	STEWART	BOAT

Homecoming

STEER	CEMETERY	MAYBETH	RETARDED	CLAIRE
BICYCLE	CRABS	MOTHER	WALLET	TOMATO
BRIDGEPORT	BOULDER	FREE SPACE	DIED	WINDOWS
SOUR	BOAT	STEWART	CRISFIELD	CAR
ANNAPOLIS	MASS	JOSEPH	LIGHT	GRANDMOTHER

Homecoming

DIED	FISH	MAP	BICYCLE	JOSEPH
WILL	MOTHER	PEGGY	CRISFIELD	BOAT
MAYBETH	STEWART	FREE SPACE	TILLERMAN	RETARDED
BOOKS	LOGAN	MASS	ROCKLAND	RUDYARD
SAMMY	GREENSLEEVES	BRIDGEPORT	WINDOWS	VERRICKER

Homecoming

SOUR	TOMATO	ANNAPOLIS	GRANDMOTHER	CLAIRE
LIGHT	STEER	WALLET	MONEY	CEMETERY
GRATEFUL	CRABS	FREE SPACE	DANNY	CAR
BOULDER	VERRICKER	WINDOWS	BRIDGEPORT	GREENSLEEVES
SAMMY	RUDYARD	ROCKLAND	MASS	LOGAN

Homecoming

GRANDMOTHER	MOTHER	MONEY	FISH	SAMMY
RUDYARD	CRISFIELD	ANNAPOLIS	TILLERMAN	BOAT
DANNY	LIGHT	FREE SPACE	CEMETERY	TOMATO
VERRICKER	MASS	BRIDGEPORT	LOGAN	WINDOWS
DIED	PEGGY	STEER	CAR	CRABS

Homecoming

STEWART	WALLET	MAYBETH	BOULDER	GRATEFUL
RETARDED	SOUR	MAP	WILL	BICYCLE
ROCKLAND	CLAIRE	FREE SPACE	JOSEPH	BOOKS
MENTAL	CRABS	CAR	STEER	PEGGY
DIED	WINDOWS	LOGAN	BRIDGEPORT	MASS

Homecoming

ANNAPOLIS	NUN	MASS	DIED	FISH
MAP	RUDYARD	CAR	BOULDER	MOTHER
BOAT	SOUR	FREE SPACE	TILLERMAN	MENTAL
PEGGY	TOMATO	WILL	BOOKS	GREENSLEEVES
DANNY	WINDOWS	BICYCLE	SAMMY	BRIDGEPORT

Homecoming

LOGAN	STEWART	WALLET	CEMETERY	LIGHT
CRABS	VERRICKER	CRISFIELD	JOSEPH	GRATEFUL
STEER	CLAIRE	FREE SPACE	MAYBETH	MONEY
GRANDMOTHER	BRIDGEPORT	SAMMY	BICYCLE	WINDOWS
DANNY	GREENSLEEVES	BOOKS	WILL	TOMATO

Homecoming

LIGHT	VERRICKER	SAMMY	ROCKLAND	SOUR
BOAT	GRANDMOTHER	DANNY	BICYCLE	WILL
DIED	JOSEPH	FREE SPACE	RETARDED	GREENSLEEVES
TILLERMAN	BOOKS	MASS	CLAIRE	BOULDER
MENTAL	PEGGY	CRISFIELD	GRATEFUL	MAYBETH

Homecoming

CEMETERY	FISH	NUN	WALLET	RUDYARD
LOGAN	MAP	MOTHER	STEER	TOMATO
ANNAPOLIS	CAR	FREE SPACE	STEWART	MONEY
CRABS	MAYBETH	GRATEFUL	CRISFIELD	PEGGY
MENTAL	BOULDER	CLAIRE	MASS	BOOKS

Homecoming Vocabulary Word List

No.	Word	Clue/Definition
1.	ABANDONED	Given up; left behind
2.	ABREAST	Side by side
3.	ABRUPTLY	Suddenly; without warning
4.	AMNESIA	Loss of memory
5.	ARCS	Shapes like curves
6.	ASKEW	To one side; awry
7.	BICKERING	Squabbling; having little quarrels
8.	BIDDABLE	Obedient; docile
9.	BOBBLING	Moving about jerkily
10.	BRISKLY	In a quick, energetic way
11.	CACOPHONY	Jarring, discordant sound
12.	CHAFED	Rubbed
13.	CIRCUITOUS	Roundabout
14.	CLAMOR	Loud outcry
15.	CLENCHED	Closed tightly
16.	COCOON	Comfortable retreat; refuge
17.	COMA	Deep, prolonged unconsciousness
18.	CONJECTURE	Guesswork
19.	CONSPICUOUS	Obvious
20.	CONTRADICTORY	Opposite of
21.	CONTRARY	Willful; perverse; ornery
22.	CONVALESCENT	Recuperating from illness or injury
23.	CONVICTION	Strong belief or opinion
24.	CROWED	Exulted loudly; boasted
25.	DABBLE	Splash
26.	DESPERATION	Despair
27.	DEVOUT	Deeply religious; sincere
28.	DINGHY	Small open boat; rowboat
29.	DRONED	Spoke in a monotonous tone
30.	DWINDLED	Became less
31.	ELABORATED	Expressed in greater detail
32.	EXASPERATED	Impatient
33.	FALTERED	Weakened; became unsteady
34.	FATIGUE	Weariness; exhaustion
35.	FLOUNCES	Gathered material attached to a skirt
36.	FLUSTERED	Made nervous or upset
37.	FRAGILE	Delicate; easily broken
38.	FURROWS	Shallow trenches made in the ground by a plow
39.	GLEAMED	Glowed
40.	GLIMPSE	See briefly
41.	GLINTING	Sparkling
42.	GNAWED	Bit; chewed on
43.	GURGLED	Make a kind of bubbling sound
44.	HEELED	Tilted
45.	HEREDITARY	Genetically transmitted
46.	HOISTED	Raised; lifted
47.	HUSTLED	Hurried along
48.	IMMOBILE	Unmoving; fixed
49.	INTENT	Concentrated; firmly fixed
50.	INTERSPERSED	Distributed randomly among
51.	LULLED	Soothed

Homecoming Vocabulary Word List Continued

No.	Word	Clue/Definition
52.	MEANDERED	Moved aimlessly and idly
53.	MIRTH	Gladness
54.	MOAT	Wide ditch filled with water
55.	MOLTEN	Made liquid and glowing
56.	MOURNFUL	Causing or suggesting sadness
57.	NAUGHTY	Mischievous
58.	ORGANDY	Stiff fabric of cotton or silk
59.	POSTPONING	Putting off until a later time
60.	PRIMLY	Properly; precisely
61.	PROD	Goad to action
62.	PUMMELED	Beat
63.	PURSED	Puckered
64.	QUELLED	Put down forcibly
65.	RAUCOUS	Rough-sounding; harsh
66.	RECITING	Repeating
67.	RETARDED	Slow in development
68.	REVERIE	State of musing; daydream
69.	REVOLVED	Turned; rotated
70.	SANCTUARY	Place of refuge
71.	SAUNTER	Walk leisurely
72.	SCOWLED	Frowned
73.	SECLUDED	Set apart
74.	SECRETIVE	Inclined to keeping secrets
75.	SIGNALS	Signs
76.	SLOUCHED	Drooped
77.	SOLEMNLY	Somberly; earnestly
78.	SOLITUDE	State of being alone
79.	STEALTHILY	Secretly
80.	STURDY	Strong; healthy
81.	SUCCEEDED	Came after
82.	SURGED	Moved up quickly; swelled
83.	SYMMETRY	Balanced or harmonious proportions
84.	TEEMING	Swarming
85.	TENACIOUS	Holding firm; stubborn
86.	TENDRILS	Twisting, threadlike shoots of a plant
87.	TENUOUS	Slight
88.	THRONGED	Crowded together
89.	TILLER	Lever that steers the boat
90.	TOUSLED	Rumpled; disheveled
91.	TRAIPSED	Walked
92.	TRESPASSING	Invading property or space of another
93.	TRUDGING	Walking laboriously
94.	TURGID	Swollen
95.	UNGODLY	Outrageous
96.	VAGUE	Lacking clear or distinct form
97.	VIBRATED	Shook; trembled
98.	VOWED	Promised solemnly; pledged
99.	WELLED	Rose up
100	ZIGZAG	Make sharp turns in alternating directions

Copyrighted

Homecoming Vocabulary Fill In The Blanks 1

_____   1. Slow in development
_____   2. Obvious
_____   3. Somberly; earnestly
_____   4. Closed tightly
_____   5. Signs
_____   6. Beat
_____   7. Raised; lifted
_____   8. Tilted
_____   9. Slight
_____   10. Rumpled; disheveled
_____   11. Comfortable retreat; refuge
_____   12. Weakened; became unsteady
_____   13. Soothed
_____   14. Place of refuge
_____   15. Side by side
_____   16. Jarring, discordant sound
_____   17. Rough-sounding; harsh
_____   18. Balanced or harmonious proportions
_____   19. Became less
_____   20. Spoke in a monotonous tone

Homecoming Vocabulary Fill In The Blanks 1 Answer Key

RETARDED	1. Slow in development
CONSPICUOUS	2. Obvious
SOLEMNLY	3. Somberly; earnestly
CLENCHED	4. Closed tightly
SIGNALS	5. Signs
PUMMELED	6. Beat
HOISTED	7. Raised; lifted
HEELED	8. Tilted
TENUOUS	9. Slight
TOUSLED	10. Rumpled; disheveled
COCOON	11. Comfortable retreat; refuge
FALTERED	12. Weakened; became unsteady
LULLED	13. Soothed
SANCTUARY	14. Place of refuge
ABREAST	15. Side by side
CACOPHONY	16. Jarring, discordant sound
RAUCOUS	17. Rough-sounding; harsh
SYMMETRY	18. Balanced or harmonious proportions
DWINDLED	19. Became less
DRONED	20. Spoke in a monotonous tone

Homecoming Vocabulary Fill In The Blanks 2

_____ 1. Made liquid and glowing

_____ 2. Slow in development

_____ 3. Walk leisurely

_____ 4. Holding firm; stubborn

_____ 5. Putting off until a later time

_____ 6. Walked

_____ 7. Impatient

_____ 8. Put down forcibly

_____ 9. Tilted

_____ 10. See briefly

_____ 11. Suddenly; without warning

_____ 12. Guesswork

_____ 13. Make sharp turns in alternating directions

_____ 14. Weakened; became unsteady

_____ 15. Shook; trembled

_____ 16. Rumpled; disheveled

_____ 17. Causing or suggesting sadness

_____ 18. Crowded together

_____ 19. Shapes like curves

_____ 20. Somberly; earnestly

Homecoming Vocabulary Fill In The Blanks 2 Answer Key

MOLTEN	1. Made liquid and glowing
RETARDED	2. Slow in development
SAUNTER	3. Walk leisurely
TENACIOUS	4. Holding firm; stubborn
POSTPONING	5. Putting off until a later time
TRAIPSED	6. Walked
EXASPERATED	7. Impatient
QUELLED	8. Put down forcibly
HEELED	9. Tilted
GLIMPSE	10. See briefly
ABRUPTLY	11. Suddenly; without warning
CONJECTURE	12. Guesswork
ZIGZAG	13. Make sharp turns in alternating directions
FALTERED	14. Weakened; became unsteady
VIBRATED	15. Shook; trembled
TOUSLED	16. Rumpled; disheveled
MOURNFUL	17. Causing or suggesting sadness
THRONGED	18. Crowded together
ARCS	19. Shapes like curves
SOLEMNLY	20. Somberly; earnestly

Homecoming Vocabulary Fill In The Blanks 3

_____ 1. Lacking clear or distinct form

_____ 2. State of being alone

_____ 3. Signs

_____ 4. Crowded together

_____ 5. In a quick, energetic way

_____ 6. Concentrated; firmly fixed

_____ 7. State of musing; daydream

_____ 8. Turned; rotated

_____ 9. Impatient

_____ 10. Twisting, threadlike shoots of a plant

_____ 11. Willful; perverse; ornery

_____ 12. Jarring, discordant sound

_____ 13. Spoke in a monotonous tone

_____ 14. Opposite of

_____ 15. Put down forcibly

_____ 16. Causing or suggesting sadness

_____ 17. Secretly

_____ 18. Sparkling

_____ 19. Comfortable retreat; refuge

_____ 20. Exulted loudly; boasted

Homecoming Vocabulary Fill In The Blanks 3 Answer Key

VAGUE	1. Lacking clear or distinct form
SOLITUDE	2. State of being alone
SIGNALS	3. Signs
THRONGED	4. Crowded together
BRISKLY	5. In a quick, energetic way
INTENT	6. Concentrated; firmly fixed
REVERIE	7. State of musing; daydream
REVOLVED	8. Turned; rotated
EXASPERATED	9. Impatient
TENDRILS	10. Twisting, threadlike shoots of a plant
CONTRARY	11. Willful; perverse; ornery
CACOPHONY	12. Jarring, discordant sound
DRONED	13. Spoke in a monotonous tone
CONTRADICTORY	14. Opposite of
QUELLED	15. Put down forcibly
MOURNFUL	16. Causing or suggesting sadness
STEALTHILY	17. Secretly
GLINTING	18. Sparkling
COCOON	19. Comfortable retreat; refuge
CROWED	20. Exulted loudly; boasted

Homecoming Vocabulary Fill In The Blanks 4

_____ 1. Guesswork

_____ 2. Twisting, threadlike shoots of a plant

_____ 3. Delicate; easily broken

_____ 4. Balanced or harmonious proportions

_____ 5. Loss of memory

_____ 6. Properly; precisely

_____ 7. Put down forcibly

_____ 8. Swarming

_____ 9. Beat

_____ 10. Despair

_____ 11. In a quick, energetic way

_____ 12. Tilted

_____ 13. Hurried along

_____ 14. Shook; trembled

_____ 15. Slight

_____ 16. Make a kind of bubbling sound

_____ 17. Side by side

_____ 18. Concentrated; firmly fixed

_____ 19. Crowded together

_____ 20. Promised solemnly; pledged

Homecoming Vocabulary Fill In The Blanks 4 Answer Key

CONJECTURE	1. Guesswork
TENDRILS	2. Twisting, threadlike shoots of a plant
FRAGILE	3. Delicate; easily broken
SYMMETRY	4. Balanced or harmonious proportions
AMNESIA	5. Loss of memory
PRIMLY	6. Properly; precisely
QUELLED	7. Put down forcibly
TEEMING	8. Swarming
PUMMELED	9. Beat
DESPERATION	10. Despair
BRISKLY	11. In a quick, energetic way
HEELED	12. Tilted
HUSTLED	13. Hurried along
VIBRATED	14. Shook; trembled
TENUOUS	15. Slight
GURGLED	16. Make a kind of bubbling sound
ABREAST	17. Side by side
INTENT	18. Concentrated; firmly fixed
THRONGED	19. Crowded together
VOWED	20. Promised solemnly; pledged

Homecoming Vocabulary Matching 1

___ 1. DRONED
___ 2. GLEAMED
___ 3. COCOON
___ 4. TENUOUS
___ 5. FLUSTERED
___ 6. FATIGUE
___ 7. CONTRADICTORY
___ 8. TRAIPSED
___ 9. WELLED
___ 10. TILLER
___ 11. GLINTING
___ 12. SUCCEEDED
___ 13. DEVOUT
___ 14. DABBLE
___ 15. CONSPICUOUS
___ 16. ZIGZAG
___ 17. SCOWLED
___ 18. TRESPASSING
___ 19. CONVALESCENT
___ 20. HUSTLED
___ 21. SECLUDED
___ 22. INTERSPERSED
___ 23. CIRCUITOUS
___ 24. CONTRARY
___ 25. RAUCOUS

A. Rose up
B. Hurried along
C. Deeply religious; sincere
D. Roundabout
E. Came after
F. Lever that steers the boat
G. Slight
H. Weariness; exhaustion
I. Walked
J. Obvious
K. Willful; perverse; ornery
L. Splash
M. Set apart
N. Sparkling
O. Distributed randomly among
P. Invading property or space of another
Q. Recuperating from illness or injury
R. Frowned
S. Opposite of
T. Glowed
U. Made nervous or upset
V. Comfortable retreat; refuge
W. Make sharp turns in alternating directions
X. Spoke in a monotonous tone
Y. Rough-sounding; harsh

Homecoming Vocabulary Matching 1 Answer Key

X - 1.	DRONED	A.	Rose up
T - 2.	GLEAMED	B.	Hurried along
V - 3.	COCOON	C.	Deeply religious; sincere
G - 4.	TENUOUS	D.	Roundabout
U - 5.	FLUSTERED	E.	Came after
H - 6.	FATIGUE	F.	Lever that steers the boat
S - 7.	CONTRADICTORY	G.	Slight
I - 8.	TRAIPSED	H.	Weariness; exhaustion
A - 9.	WELLED	I.	Walked
F - 10.	TILLER	J.	Obvious
N - 11.	GLINTING	K.	Willful; perverse; ornery
E - 12.	SUCCEEDED	L.	Splash
C - 13.	DEVOUT	M.	Set apart
L - 14.	DABBLE	N.	Sparkling
J - 15.	CONSPICUOUS	O.	Distributed randomly among
W - 16.	ZIGZAG	P.	Invading property or space of another
R - 17.	SCOWLED	Q.	Recuperating from illness or injury
P - 18.	TRESPASSING	R.	Frowned
Q - 19.	CONVALESCENT	S.	Opposite of
B - 20.	HUSTLED	T.	Glowed
M - 21.	SECLUDED	U.	Made nervous or upset
O - 22.	INTERSPERSED	V.	Comfortable retreat; refuge
D - 23.	CIRCUITOUS	W.	Make sharp turns in alternating directions
K - 24.	CONTRARY	X.	Spoke in a monotonous tone
Y - 25.	RAUCOUS	Y.	Rough-sounding; harsh

Homecoming Vocabulary Matching 2

___ 1. MOURNFUL
___ 2. FATIGUE
___ 3. TEEMING
___ 4. CIRCUITOUS
___ 5. EXASPERATED
___ 6. MOLTEN
___ 7. TOUSLED
___ 8. REVOLVED
___ 9. SAUNTER
___10. PROD
___11. GLINTING
___12. NAUGHTY
___13. TILLER
___14. BIDDABLE
___15. ARCS
___16. HOISTED
___17. SECLUDED
___18. ORGANDY
___19. VAGUE
___20. RAUCOUS
___21. CONTRADICTORY
___22. BRISKLY
___23. RETARDED
___24. MEANDERED
___25. PUMMELED

A. Swarming
B. Goad to action
C. Stiff fabric of cotton or silk
D. Walk leisurely
E. Raised; lifted
F. Beat
G. Causing or suggesting sadness
H. Opposite of
I. Rumpled; disheveled
J. Turned; rotated
K. Mischievous
L. Slow in development
M. Set apart
N. Shapes like curves
O. Weariness; exhaustion
P. Rough-sounding; harsh
Q. In a quick, energetic way
R. Impatient
S. Made liquid and glowing
T. Obedient; docile
U. Roundabout
V. Moved aimlessly and idly
W. Lever that steers the boat
X. Lacking clear or distinct form
Y. Sparkling

Homecoming Vocabulary Matching 2 Answer Key

G - 1. MOURNFUL	A.	Swarming
O - 2. FATIGUE	B.	Goad to action
A - 3. TEEMING	C.	Stiff fabric of cotton or silk
U - 4. CIRCUITOUS	D.	Walk leisurely
R - 5. EXASPERATED	E.	Raised; lifted
S - 6. MOLTEN	F.	Beat
I - 7. TOUSLED	G.	Causing or suggesting sadness
J - 8. REVOLVED	H.	Opposite of
D - 9. SAUNTER	I.	Rumpled; disheveled
B - 10. PROD	J.	Turned; rotated
Y - 11. GLINTING	K.	Mischievous
K - 12. NAUGHTY	L.	Slow in development
W - 13. TILLER	M.	Set apart
T - 14. BIDDABLE	N.	Shapes like curves
N - 15. ARCS	O.	Weariness; exhaustion
E - 16. HOISTED	P.	Rough-sounding; harsh
M - 17. SECLUDED	Q.	In a quick, energetic way
C - 18. ORGANDY	R.	Impatient
X - 19. VAGUE	S.	Made liquid and glowing
P - 20. RAUCOUS	T.	Obedient; docile
H - 21. CONTRADICTORY	U.	Roundabout
Q - 22. BRISKLY	V.	Moved aimlessly and idly
L - 23. RETARDED	W.	Lever that steers the boat
V - 24. MEANDERED	X.	Lacking clear or distinct form
F - 25. PUMMELED	Y.	Sparkling

Homecoming Vocabulary Matching 3

___ 1. DINGHY   A. Place of refuge
___ 2. FURROWS   B. Small open boat; rowboat
___ 3. DABBLE   C. Signs
___ 4. TILLER   D. Stiff fabric of cotton or silk
___ 5. ELABORATED   E. Moved up quickly; swelled
___ 6. CLENCHED   F. Moved aimlessly and idly
___ 7. TENACIOUS   G. Raised; lifted
___ 8. ABRUPTLY   H. Expressed in greater detail
___ 9. VOWED   I. Splash
___ 10. UNGODLY   J. Lever that steers the boat
___ 11. CACOPHONY   K. Holding firm; stubborn
___ 12. ORGANDY   L. Weariness; exhaustion
___ 13. HOISTED   M. Shallow trenches made in the ground by a plow
___ 14. SANCTUARY   N. Walk leisurely
___ 15. MEANDERED   O. Bit; chewed on
___ 16. SOLEMNLY   P. Somberly; earnestly
___ 17. MOLTEN   Q. Outrageous
___ 18. CONTRARY   R. Despair
___ 19. SAUNTER   S. Promised solemnly; pledged
___ 20. SURGED   T. Willful; perverse; ornery
___ 21. GNAWED   U. Rumpled; disheveled
___ 22. DESPERATION   V. Jarring, discordant sound
___ 23. FATIGUE   W. Suddenly; without warning
___ 24. TOUSLED   X. Made liquid and glowing
___ 25. SIGNALS   Y. Closed tightly

Homecoming Vocabulary Matching 3 Answer Key

B - 1. DINGHY	A.	Place of refuge
M - 2. FURROWS	B.	Small open boat; rowboat
I - 3. DABBLE	C.	Signs
J - 4. TILLER	D.	Stiff fabric of cotton or silk
H - 5. ELABORATED	E.	Moved up quickly; swelled
Y - 6. CLENCHED	F.	Moved aimlessly and idly
K - 7. TENACIOUS	G.	Raised; lifted
W - 8. ABRUPTLY	H.	Expressed in greater detail
S - 9. VOWED	I.	Splash
Q - 10. UNGODLY	J.	Lever that steers the boat
V - 11. CACOPHONY	K.	Holding firm; stubborn
D - 12. ORGANDY	L.	Weariness; exhaustion
G - 13. HOISTED	M.	Shallow trenches made in the ground by a plow
A - 14. SANCTUARY	N.	Walk leisurely
F - 15. MEANDERED	O.	Bit; chewed on
P - 16. SOLEMNLY	P.	Somberly; earnestly
X - 17. MOLTEN	Q.	Outrageous
T - 18. CONTRARY	R.	Despair
N - 19. SAUNTER	S.	Promised solemnly; pledged
E - 20. SURGED	T.	Willful; perverse; ornery
O - 21. GNAWED	U.	Rumpled; disheveled
R - 22. DESPERATION	V.	Jarring, discordant sound
L - 23. FATIGUE	W.	Suddenly; without warning
U - 24. TOUSLED	X.	Made liquid and glowing
C - 25. SIGNALS	Y.	Closed tightly

Homecoming Vocabulary Matching 4

___ 1. QUELLED
___ 2. FRAGILE
___ 3. AMNESIA
___ 4. UNGODLY
___ 5. CONJECTURE
___ 6. LULLED
___ 7. INTERSPERSED
___ 8. TRESPASSING
___ 9. ASKEW
___ 10. RECITING
___ 11. MIRTH
___ 12. CLENCHED
___ 13. SECRETIVE
___ 14. FLOUNCES
___ 15. NAUGHTY
___ 16. COCOON
___ 17. RETARDED
___ 18. MEANDERED
___ 19. CONVICTION
___ 20. GLIMPSE
___ 21. SOLITUDE
___ 22. STURDY
___ 23. FLUSTERED
___ 24. EXASPERATED
___ 25. CACOPHONY

A. See briefly
B. Invading property or space of another
C. Put down forcibly
D. Outrageous
E. Loss of memory
F. Strong belief or opinion
G. Gathered material attached to a skirt
H. Delicate; easily broken
I. Inclined to keeping secrets
J. Repeating
K. State of being alone
L. Closed tightly
M. Soothed
N. Distributed randomly among
O. Gladness
P. Slow in development
Q. Strong; healthy
R. Guesswork
S. Made nervous or upset
T. Impatient
U. Jarring, discordant sound
V. Moved aimlessly and idly
W. Comfortable retreat; refuge
X. To one side; awry
Y. Mischievous

Homecoming Vocabulary Matching 4 Answer Key

C - 1. QUELLED	A.	See briefly
H - 2. FRAGILE	B.	Invading property or space of another
E - 3. AMNESIA	C.	Put down forcibly
D - 4. UNGODLY	D.	Outrageous
R - 5. CONJECTURE	E.	Loss of memory
M - 6. LULLED	F.	Strong belief or opinion
N - 7. INTERSPERSED	G.	Gathered material attached to a skirt
B - 8. TRESPASSING	H.	Delicate; easily broken
X - 9. ASKEW	I.	Inclined to keeping secrets
J - 10. RECITING	J.	Repeating
O - 11. MIRTH	K.	State of being alone
L - 12. CLENCHED	L.	Closed tightly
I - 13. SECRETIVE	M.	Soothed
G - 14. FLOUNCES	N.	Distributed randomly among
Y - 15. NAUGHTY	O.	Gladness
W - 16. COCOON	P.	Slow in development
P - 17. RETARDED	Q.	Strong; healthy
V - 18. MEANDERED	R.	Guesswork
F - 19. CONVICTION	S.	Made nervous or upset
A - 20. GLIMPSE	T.	Impatient
K - 21. SOLITUDE	U.	Jarring, discordant sound
Q - 22. STURDY	V.	Moved aimlessly and idly
S - 23. FLUSTERED	W.	Comfortable retreat; refuge
T - 24. EXASPERATED	X.	To one side; awry
U - 25. CACOPHONY	Y.	Mischievous

Homecoming Vocabulary Magic Squares 1

Match the definition with the vocabulary word. Put your answers in the magic squares below. When your answers are correct, all columns and rows will add to the same number.

A. NAUGHTY
B. TILLER
C. TENACIOUS
D. REVERIE
E. TENDRILS
F. COMA
G. TOUSLED
H. SOLITUDE
I. STEALTHILY
J. SCOWLED
K. BOBBLING
L. CONJECTURE
M. ASKEW
N. ORGANDY
O. SYMMETRY
P. DRONED

1. Holding firm; stubborn
2. Frowned
3. Deep, prolonged unconsciousness
4. Balanced or harmonious proportions
5. Spoke in a monotonous tone
6. Twisting, threadlike shoots of a plant
7. Secretly
8. State of musing; daydream
9. To one side; awry
10. State of being alone
11. Guesswork
12. Mischievous
13. Lever that steers the boat
14. Moving about jerkily
15. Rumpled; disheveled
16. Stiff fabric of cotton or silk

A=	B=	C=	D=
E=	F=	G=	H=
I=	J=	K=	L=
M=	N=	O=	P=

Homecoming Vocabulary Magic Squares 1 Answer Key

Match the definition with the vocabulary word. Put your answers in the magic squares below. When your answers are correct, all columns and rows will add to the same number.

A. NAUGHTY
B. TILLER
C. TENACIOUS
D. REVERIE
E. TENDRILS
F. COMA
G. TOUSLED
H. SOLITUDE
I. STEALTHILY
J. SCOWLED
K. BOBBLING
L. CONJECTURE
M. ASKEW
N. ORGANDY
O. SYMMETRY
P. DRONED

1. Holding firm; stubborn
2. Frowned
3. Deep, prolonged unconsciousness
4. Balanced or harmonious proportions
5. Spoke in a monotonous tone
6. Twisting, threadlike shoots of a plant
7. Secretly
8. State of musing; daydream
9. To one side; awry
10. State of being alone
11. Guesswork
12. Mischievous
13. Lever that steers the boat
14. Moving about jerkily
15. Rumpled; disheveled
16. Stiff fabric of cotton or silk

A=12	B=13	C=1	D=8
E=6	F=3	G=15	H=10
I=7	J=2	K=14	L=11
M=9	N=16	O=4	P=5

Homecoming Vocabulary Magic Squares 2

Match the definition with the vocabulary word. Put your answers in the magic squares below. When your answers are correct, all columns and rows will add to the same number.

A. PURSED
B. GURGLED
C. CONTRARY
D. GLIMPSE
E. MOLTEN
F. VAGUE
G. VOWED
H. CONVALESCENT
I. FLUSTERED
J. FATIGUE
K. GLEAMED
L. SIGNALS
M. TENDRILS
N. DINGHY
O. CLAMOR
P. AMNESIA

1. Puckered
2. Small open boat; rowboat
3. Weariness; exhaustion
4. Made liquid and glowing
5. Promised solemnly; pledged
6. Signs
7. Loss of memory
8. Willful; perverse; ornery
9. Loud outcry
10. See briefly
11. Recuperating from illness or injury
12. Glowed
13. Made nervous or upset
14. Lacking clear or distinct form
15. Make a kind of bubbling sound
16. Twisting, threadlike shoots of a plant

A=	B=	C=	D=
E=	F=	G=	H=
I=	J=	K=	L=
M=	N=	O=	P=

81
Copyrighted

Homecoming Vocabulary Magic Squares 2 Answer Key

Match the definition with the vocabulary word. Put your answers in the magic squares below. When your answers are correct, all columns and rows will add to the same number.

A. PURSED
B. GURGLED
C. CONTRARY
D. GLIMPSE
E. MOLTEN
F. VAGUE
G. VOWED
H. CONVALESCENT
I. FLUSTERED
J. FATIGUE
K. GLEAMED
L. SIGNALS
M. TENDRILS
N. DINGHY
O. CLAMOR
P. AMNESIA

1. Puckered
2. Small open boat; rowboat
3. Weariness; exhaustion
4. Made liquid and glowing
5. Promised solemnly; pledged
6. Signs
7. Loss of memory
8. Willful; perverse; ornery
9. Loud outcry
10. See briefly
11. Recuperating from illness or injury
12. Glowed
13. Made nervous or upset
14. Lacking clear or distinct form
15. Make a kind of bubbling sound
16. Twisting, threadlike shoots of a plant

A=1	B=15	C=8	D=10
E=4	F=14	G=5	H=11
I=13	J=3	K=12	L=6
M=16	N=2	O=9	P=7

Homecoming Vocabulary Magic Squares 3

Match the definition with the vocabulary word. Put your answers in the magic squares below. When your answers are correct, all columns and rows will add to the same number.

A. FLUSTERED
B. CROWED
C. AMNESIA
D. HEELED
E. VOWED
F. DEVOUT

G. CONTRARY
H. DABBLE
I. VIBRATED
J. CONTRADICTORY
K. HUSTLED
L. GLEAMED

M. SYMMETRY
N. HOISTED
O. SOLEMNLY
P. PRIMLY

1. Somberly; earnestly
2. Opposite of
3. Splash
4. Made nervous or upset
5. Tilted
6. Promised solemnly; pledged
7. Hurried along
8. Raised; lifted
9. Deeply religious; sincere
10. Loss of memory
11. Balanced or harmonious proportions
12. Glowed
13. Shook; trembled
14. Properly; precisely
15. Exulted loudly; boasted
16. Willful; perverse; ornery

A=	B=	C=	D=
E=	F=	G=	H=
I=	J=	K=	L=
M=	N=	O=	P=

Homecoming Vocabulary Magic Squares 3 Answer Key

Match the definition with the vocabulary word. Put your answers in the magic squares below. When your answers are correct, all columns and rows will add to the same number.

A. FLUSTERED
B. CROWED
C. AMNESIA
D. HEELED
E. VOWED
F. DEVOUT
G. CONTRARY
H. DABBLE
I. VIBRATED
J. CONTRADICTORY
K. HUSTLED
L. GLEAMED
M. SYMMETRY
N. HOISTED
O. SOLEMNLY
P. PRIMLY

1. Somberly; earnestly
2. Opposite of
3. Splash
4. Made nervous or upset
5. Tilted
6. Promised solemnly; pledged
7. Hurried along
8. Raised; lifted
9. Deeply religious; sincere
10. Loss of memory
11. Balanced or harmonious proportions
12. Glowed
13. Shook; trembled
14. Properly; precisely
15. Exulted loudly; boasted
16. Willful; perverse; ornery

A=4	B=15	C=10	D=5
E=6	F=9	G=16	H=3
I=13	J=2	K=7	L=12
M=11	N=8	O=1	P=14

Homecoming Vocabulary Magic Squares 4

Match the definition with the vocabulary word. Put your answers in the magic squares below. When your answers are correct, all columns and rows will add to the same number.

A. TOUSLED
B. SURGED
C. ZIGZAG
D. STURDY
E. GNAWED
F. REVERIE
G. TENUOUS
H. RETARDED
I. CACOPHONY
J. CROWED
K. COMA
L. CLENCHED
M. PROD
N. TENACIOUS
O. ABANDONED
P. CONTRADICTORY

1. Slow in development
2. Rumpled; disheveled
3. Moved up quickly; swelled
4. Slight
5. Exulted loudly; boasted
6. Given up; left behind
7. Opposite of
8. Jarring, discordant sound
9. Deep, prolonged unconsciousness
10. Holding firm; stubborn
11. Goad to action
12. Closed tightly
13. Bit; chewed on
14. Strong; healthy
15. Make sharp turns in alternating directions
16. State of musing; daydream

A=	B=	C=	D=
E=	F=	G=	H=
I=	J=	K=	L=
M=	N=	O=	P=

Homecoming Vocabulary Magic Squares 4 Answer Key

Match the definition with the vocabulary word. Put your answers in the magic squares below. When your answers are correct, all columns and rows will add to the same number.

A. TOUSLED
B. SURGED
C. ZIGZAG
D. STURDY
E. GNAWED
F. REVERIE
G. TENUOUS
H. RETARDED
I. CACOPHONY
J. CROWED
K. COMA
L. CLENCHED
M. PROD
N. TENACIOUS
O. ABANDONED
P. CONTRADICTORY

1. Slow in development
2. Rumpled; disheveled
3. Moved up quickly; swelled
4. Slight
5. Exulted loudly; boasted
6. Given up; left behind
7. Opposite of
8. Jarring, discordant sound
9. Deep, prolonged unconsciousness
10. Holding firm; stubborn
11. Goad to action
12. Closed tightly
13. Bit; chewed on
14. Strong; healthy
15. Make sharp turns in alternating directions
16. State of musing; daydream

A=2	B=3	C=15	D=14
E=13	F=16	G=4	H=1
I=8	J=5	K=9	L=12
M=11	N=10	O=6	P=7

Homecoming Vocabulary Word Search 1

```
C O C O O N S E C N U O L F S S D Q C S V
O L Q Z K P I U F Z Y V J Q U Y T U L U Z
M B E M S R D G A D I A K O R M M E A R D
A H F N E S S I L E C G C D G M D L M G M
M T B V C C S T W J U Z N M E M L O E S
E H E J R H T A E O A E I A L T Q E R D O
A R A A E A E F R R G D E G R M D F D L
N O M S T F A D E C D E M D C Y S O E P E
D N N E I E L V D U V M E D G I L L A Z M
E G E C V D T Q R O U S F T G T E G M T N
R E S L E F H T U P R D N N O E H B I Y L
E D I U R R I T T U I G A R H U U R R V Y
D U A D U A L V P G G L A B G H S Q T O M
G T H E T G Y M R W S Y P N B Z T L H W A
L I G D C I D U O L U L L E D L L D E E B
I L N Z E L T F G L P R I M L Y E Q D D R
M O A R J E F L U S T E R E D N D D O F E
P S W U N G O D L Y T E N U O U S R M P A
S D E E N O D N A B A H Z N R K H P T W P S
E T D S C O W L E D D E D R A T E R W S T
```

Balanced or harmonious proportions (8)
Beat (8)
Bit; chewed on (6)
Closed tightly (8)
Comfortable retreat; refuge (6)
Crowded together (8)
Deep, prolonged unconsciousness (4)
Deeply religious; sincere (6)
Delicate; easily broken (7)
Exulted loudly; boasted (6)
Frowned (7)
Gathered material attached to a skirt (8)
Given up; left behind (9)
Gladness (5)
Goad to action (4)
Guesswork (10)
Hurried along (7)
Inclined to keeping secrets (9)
Lacking clear or distinct form (5)
Loss of memory (7)
Loud outcry (6)
Made liquid and glowing (6)
Made nervous or upset (9)
Make sharp turns in alternating directions (6)
Moved aimlessly and idly (9)
Moved up quickly; swelled (6)
Outrageous (7)
Promised solemnly; pledged (5)

Properly; precisely (6)
Puckered (6)
Put down forcibly (7)
Rough-sounding; harsh (7)
Rubbed (6)
Rumpled; disheveled (7)
Secretly (10)
See briefly (7)
Set apart (8)
Shapes like curves (4)
Side by side (7)
Signs (7)
Slight (7)
Slow in development (8)
Somberly; earnestly (8)
Soothed (6)
Splash (6)
Spoke in a monotonous tone (6)
State of being alone (8)
State of musing; daydream (7)
Stiff fabric of cotton or silk (7)
Swollen (6)
Tilted (6)
Walking laboriously (8)
Weakened; became unsteady (8)
Weariness; exhaustion (7)
Wide ditch filled with water (4)

Homecoming Vocabulary Word Search 1 Answer Key

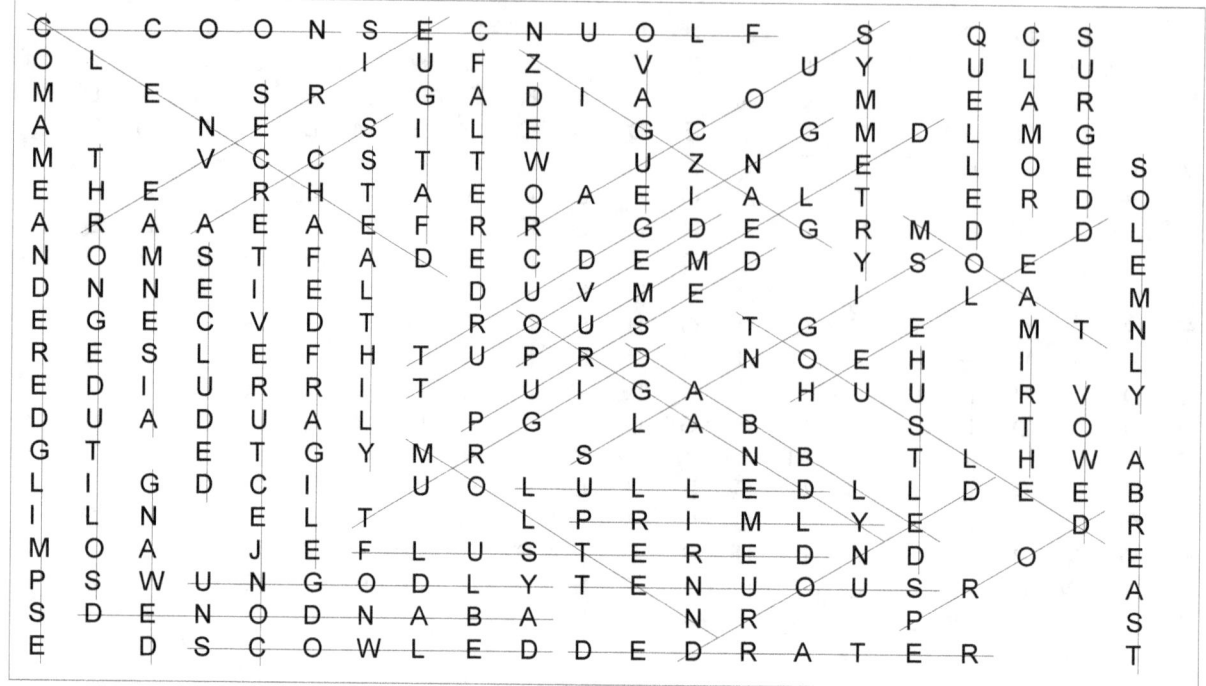

Balanced or harmonious proportions (8)
Beat (8)
Bit; chewed on (6)
Closed tightly (8)
Comfortable retreat; refuge (6)
Crowded together (8)
Deep, prolonged unconsciousness (4)
Deeply religious; sincere (6)
Delicate; easily broken (7)
Exulted loudly; boasted (6)
Frowned (7)
Gathered material attached to a skirt (8)
Given up; left behind (9)
Gladness (5)
Goad to action (4)
Guesswork (10)
Hurried along (7)
Inclined to keeping secrets (9)
Lacking clear or distinct form (5)
Loss of memory (7)
Loud outcry (6)
Made liquid and glowing (6)
Made nervous or upset (9)
Make sharp turns in alternating directions (6)
Moved aimlessly and idly (9)
Moved up quickly; swelled (6)
Outrageous (7)
Promised solemnly; pledged (5)

Properly; precisely (6)
Puckered (6)
Put down forcibly (7)
Rough-sounding; harsh (7)
Rubbed (6)
Rumpled; disheveled (7)
Secretly (10)
See briefly (7)
Set apart (8)
Shapes like curves (4)
Side by side (7)
Signs (7)
Slight (7)
Slow in development (8)
Somberly; earnestly (8)
Soothed (6)
Splash (6)
Spoke in a monotonous tone (6)
State of being alone (8)
State of musing; daydream (7)
Stiff fabric of cotton or silk (7)
Swollen (6)
Tilted (6)
Walking laboriously (8)
Weakened; became unsteady (8)
Weariness; exhaustion (7)
Wide ditch filled with water (4)

Homecoming Vocabulary Word Search 2

```
J V C S U O U C I P S N O C S B C T I W T
W U A L R T H R O N G E D N O G O R N X R
D N B R E L I T N D H S J L L C U T X A
I G R Q T N V P K M T A F B E I O D E X I
G O E P A P C K Z E Y R B D M M O G N M P
R D A U R D V H Y A L G A B N P N I T Y S
U L S R D A I S E N M A B R L S D N H E E
T Y T S E H E R E D I T A R Y E N G C F D
E R C E D G E Y E E R Q M D W E N N I A E
X R E D N T P L U R P B R O T I U H R L N
A S L S N U L G G E S U R L D O R P C T O
S H B U P E O Y A D T C O W L S A D U E D
P U A F W A M U V S E M O F J U S R I R N
E S D Q L S S I S I L V M W K C K O T E A
R T D L C U S S R P W C O H L C E N O D B
A L I Q O R L E I T C L A W C E W E U T A
T E B C M G V L D N H A T C E E D D S N G
E D U K A E G N E F G M D E L D N I W D P
D A D X R D M D G D G O X H E E L E D V V
R G L E A M E D Y Z J R M R N D E V O U T
```

Became less (8)
Came after (9)
Closed tightly (8)
Comfortable retreat; refuge (6)
Concentrated; firmly fixed (6)
Crowded together (8)
Deep, prolonged unconsciousness (4)
Deeply religious; sincere (6)
Exulted loudly; boasted (6)
Frowned (7)
Gathered material attached to a skirt (8)
Genetically transmitted (10)
Given up; left behind (9)
Gladness (5)
Glowed (7)
Goad to action (4)
Hurried along (7)
Impatient (11)
Invading property or space of another (11)
Lacking clear or distinct form (5)
Lever that steers the boat (6)
Loss of memory (7)
Loud outcry (6)
Made liquid and glowing (6)
Moved aimlessly and idly (9)
Moved up quickly; swelled (6)
Obedient; docile (8)
Obvious (11)

Outrageous (7)
Promised solemnly; pledged (5)
Properly; precisely (6)
Puckered (6)
Rose up (6)
Rough-sounding; harsh (7)
Roundabout (10)
See briefly (7)
Shapes like curves (4)
Side by side (7)
Slight (7)
Slow in development (8)
Small open boat; rowboat (6)
Somberly; earnestly (8)
Soothed (6)
Splash (6)
Spoke in a monotonous tone (6)
State of musing; daydream (7)
Strong; healthy (6)
Swollen (6)
Tilted (6)
To one side; awry (5)
Walk leisurely (7)
Walked (8)
Walking laboriously (8)
Weakened; became unsteady (8)
Wide ditch filled with water (4)
Willful; perverse; ornery (8)

Homecoming Vocabulary Word Search 2 Answer Key

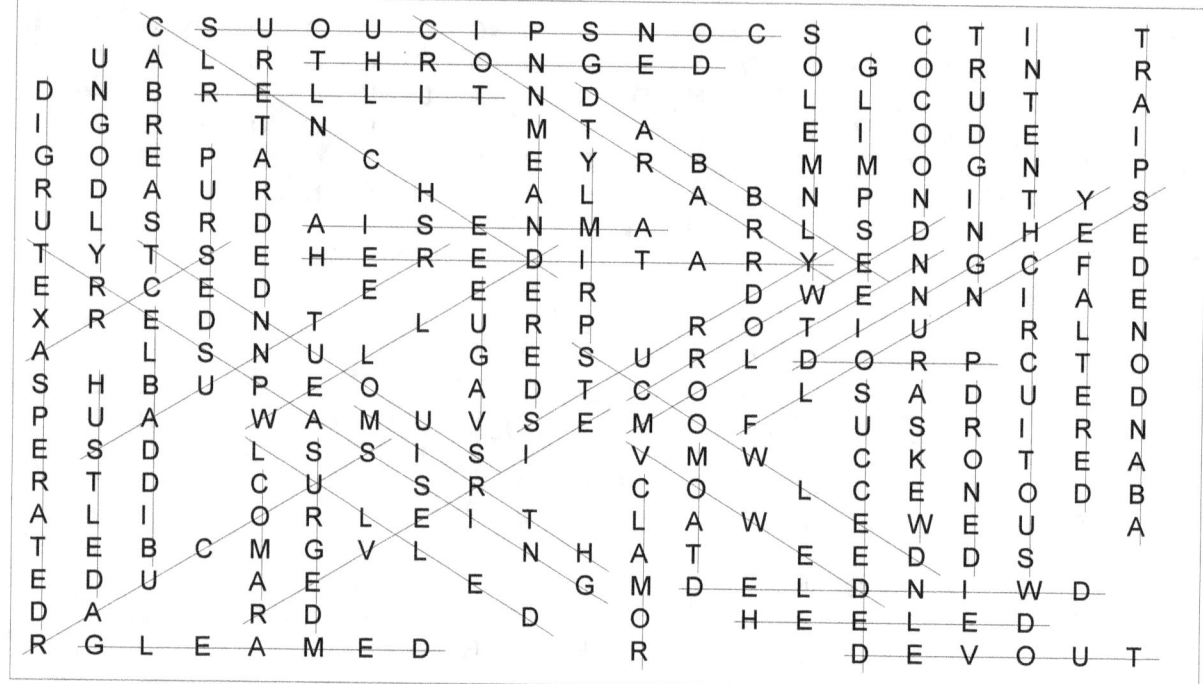

Became less (8)
Came after (9)
Closed tightly (8)
Comfortable retreat; refuge (6)
Concentrated; firmly fixed (6)
Crowded together (8)
Deep, prolonged unconsciousness (4)
Deeply religious; sincere (6)
Exulted loudly; boasted (6)
Frowned (7)
Gathered material attached to a skirt (8)
Genetically transmitted (10)
Given up; left behind (9)
Gladness (5)
Glowed (7)
Goad to action (4)
Hurried along (7)
Impatient (11)
Invading property or space of another (11)
Lacking clear or distinct form (5)
Lever that steers the boat (6)
Loss of memory (7)
Loud outcry (6)
Made liquid and glowing (6)
Moved aimlessly and idly (9)
Moved up quickly; swelled (6)
Obedient; docile (8)
Obvious (11)

Outrageous (7)
Promised solemnly; pledged (5)
Properly; precisely (6)
Puckered (6)
Rose up (6)
Rough-sounding; harsh (7)
Roundabout (10)
See briefly (7)
Shapes like curves (4)
Side by side (7)
Slight (7)
Slow in development (8)
Small open boat; rowboat (6)
Somberly; earnestly (8)
Soothed (6)
Splash (6)
Spoke in a monotonous tone (6)
State of musing; daydream (7)
Strong; healthy (6)
Swollen (6)
Tilted (6)
To one side; awry (5)
Walk leisurely (7)
Walked (8)
Walking laboriously (8)
Weakened; became unsteady (8)
Wide ditch filled with water (4)
Willful; perverse; ornery (8)

Homecoming Vocabulary Word Search 3

```
S E C R E T I V E L C R O W E D H A A F F
E L M O E C A T M H A O F N M H B B A U
C A G M H V B R A O C G M R Y D R R L R
L B N A I E R F C O F J A F H E U T R
U O I L Q R E R E S P M I L G D A P E O
D R G C T D T L I T H Z O R N E S T R W
E A D G K R D H E E O U Y I G F T L E S
D T U N D E N O R D N D T R R D A J Y D A
N E R E L L R S P C Y N U E T O R J S E U
A D T T Q L A I E C I S T M Q Y T P S N
U P S L U I I S N L P A U H B C E H Y R T
G U D O E T S M G G R A M D X A O M H E
H M A M L G E R P D G E K E L T M C G P R
T M B M L E N P E I A S X T R E V G O E K
Y E B D E V M D N H J H A C A A L O I
V L L E D R A N D G D I I R Y Z T I G N
O E E V D Z Q E L H L P Y B G K G N T U Z
W D C O N T R A R Y S U O I C N E T F E
E Z R U D E R V P E T V Z V R G N A W E D
D P H T D T E N D R I L S F Q T A S K E W
```

ABREAST	CROWED	GNAWED	PUMMELED	TENACIOUS
ABRUPTLY	DABBLE	HEELED	PURSED	TENDRILS
AMNESIA	DEVOUT	HEREDITARY	QUELLED	TILLER
ARCS	DINGHY	HOISTED	RETARDED	TRAIPSED
ASKEW	DRONED	HUSTLED	REVERIE	TRUDGING
BICKERING	ELABORATED	INTENT	SAUNTER	TURGID
CACOPHONY	FALTERED	MEANDERED	SECLUDED	VAGUE
CHAFED	FLOUNCES	MIRTH	SECRETIVE	VIBRATED
CLAMOR	FRAGILE	MOAT	SOLEMNLY	VOWED
COCOON	FURROWS	MOLTEN	STEALTHILY	ZIGZAG
COMA	GLIMPSE	NAUGHTY	SURGED	
CONTRARY	GLINTING	PROD	SYMMETRY	

Homecoming Vocabulary Word Search 3 Answer Key

ABREAST	CROWED	GNAWED	PUMMELED	TENACIOUS
ABRUPTLY	DABBLE	HEELED	PURSED	TENDRILS
AMNESIA	DEVOUT	HEREDITARY	QUELLED	TILLER
ARCS	DINGHY	HOISTED	RETARDED	TRAIPSED
ASKEW	DRONED	HUSTLED	REVERIE	TRUDGING
BICKERING	ELABORATED	INTENT	SAUNTER	TURGID
CACOPHONY	FALTERED	MEANDERED	SECLUDED	VAGUE
CHAFED	FLOUNCES	MIRTH	SECRETIVE	VIBRATED
CLAMOR	FRAGILE	MOAT	SOLEMNLY	VOWED
COCOON	FURROWS	MOLTEN	STEALTHILY	ZIGZAG
COMA	GLIMPSE	NAUGHTY	SURGED	
CONTRARY	GLINTING	PROD	SYMMETRY	

Homecoming Vocabulary Word Search 4

```
G N I M E E T R A I P S E D E L L E U Q V
L E P Q R O M A L C L A L P X T L M H O S
I X O T G Z J G L U I C B U T K U B O O A
M A S F I D I V Y G C A O G N W O A L I N
P S T V T L X G A N D O T N S T V T S C C
S P P H A F L R Z D U J U A B E D E T T T
E E O R F G F E I A N Y R S U R D R N E U
D R N S I T U B R P G L G K R C A G P D A
S A I C S M M E C S O T I E D D L R N H R
T T N O U S L R T Y D P D W Y E Z Z Y E Y
E E G W R K O Y C M L U Y N V G X L D E T
A D Y L G W G L N M Y R F S L N G E C L D
L D L E E W L D I E A B B U P O D V S E R
T E N D D D E R E T L A F U R R O W S D E
H D M C N W A L I R U N Z M A H O R C I C
I U E Z O L M D T Y R D D T P T U D R H I
L L L V X K E X A U N F E D W P J E A T T
Y C O M A R D Y O A B R E A S T V F L R I
F E S D E L E M M U P V Y X D E E F G I N
M S Q H S I G N A L S S L I R D N E T M G
```

ABREAST
ABRUPTLY
ARCS
ASKEW
BIDDABLE
CHAFED
CLAMOR
COMA
CONTRARY
CROWED
DABBLE
DEVOUT
EXASPERATED
FALTERED
FATIGUE

FRAGILE
FURROWS
GLEAMED
GLIMPSE
HEELED
HEREDITARY
HOISTED
MIRTH
MOAT
MOLTEN
MOURNFUL
POSTPONING
PRIMLY
PROD
PUMMELED

PURSED
QUELLED
RAUCOUS
RECITING
RETARDED
REVERIE
SANCTUARY
SAUNTER
SCOWLED
SECLUDED
SIGNALS
SOLEMNLY
SOLITUDE
STEALTHILY
STURDY

SURGED
SYMMETRY
TEEMING
TENDRILS
THRONGED
TILLER
TRAIPSED
TURGID
UNGODLY
VAGUE
VOWED
ZIGZAG

Homecoming Vocabulary Word Search 4 Answer Key

```
G N I M E E T R A I P S E D E L L E U Q
L E P U R O M A L C L A L T L M O H S
I X O T G Z U I C A B U O B O I A
M A S T I G C A T O N B D I N
P S T V I L G A D U N T R T O S C
S E P O R F G F E I A Y R A R D R E T
  E R O S I U B R U G S D D N U
S A N C S M E C S O L K E G E A
T T I O O S R Y D P I W Y N L R
E E N G W G O Y M Y R Y D E Y
A D Y L E L D I E A B U P O D E D
L D N D D E R E T L A F U R R O W S I
T E M   W A   I   T   N A H O C T
H D M     M T     Y   R D T U D R A
I U E   O     E   A U     P E E H I
L L L       M D           E     F R T
Y C O M A R D O A B R E A S T V R I
  E S D E L E M M U P         E E N
  S H S I G N A L S S L I R D N E T M G
```

ABREAST	FRAGILE	PURSED	SURGED
ABRUPTLY	FURROWS	QUELLED	SYMMETRY
ARCS	GLEAMED	RAUCOUS	TEEMING
ASKEW	GLIMPSE	RECITING	TENDRILS
BIDDABLE	HEELED	RETARDED	THRONGED
CHAFED	HEREDITARY	REVERIE	TILLER
CLAMOR	HOISTED	SANCTUARY	TRAIPSED
COMA	MIRTH	SAUNTER	TURGID
CONTRARY	MOAT	SCOWLED	UNGODLY
CROWED	MOLTEN	SECLUDED	VAGUE
DABBLE	MOURNFUL	SIGNALS	VOWED
DEVOUT	POSTPONING	SOLEMNLY	ZIGZAG
EXASPERATED	PRIMLY	SOLITUDE	
FALTERED	PROD	STEALTHILY	
FATIGUE	PUMMELED	STURDY	

Copyrighted

Homecoming Vocabulary Crossword 1

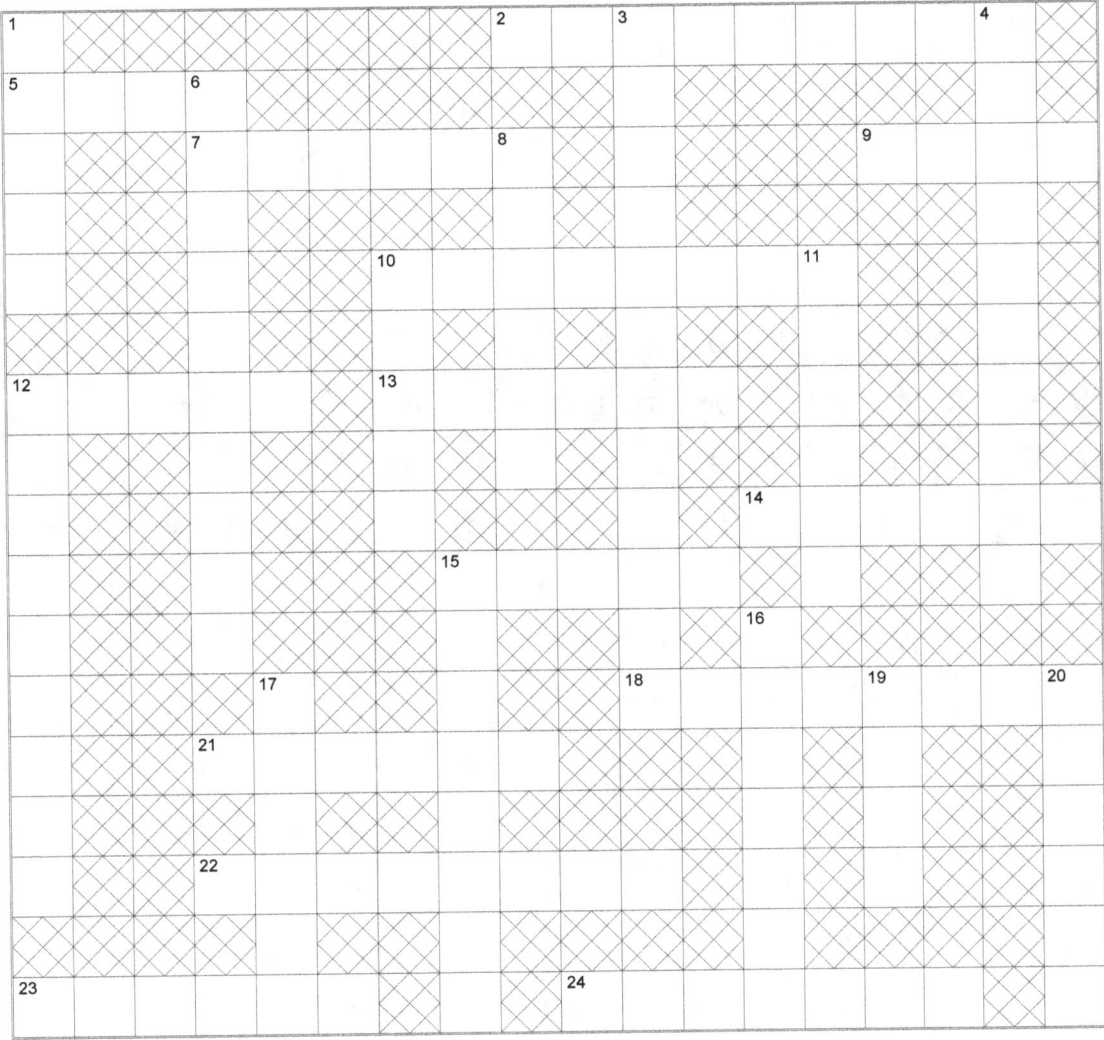

Across
2. Inclined to keeping secrets
5. Shapes like curves
7. Swollen
9. Wide ditch filled with water
10. Shook; trembled
12. Gladness
13. Rose up
14. Rubbed
15. To one side; awry
18. Walked
21. Deeply religious; sincere
22. Sparkling
23. Strong; healthy
24. Shallow trenches made in the ground by a plow

Down
1. Lacking clear or distinct form
3. Recuperating from illness or injury
4. Expressed in greater detail
6. Secretly
8. Splash
10. Promised solemnly; pledged
11. Small open boat; rowboat
12. Moved aimlessly and idly
15. Suddenly; without warning
16. Walk leisurely
17. Tilted
19. Goad to action
20. Spoke in a monotonous tone

Homecoming Vocabulary Crossword 1 Answer Key

Across
- 2. Inclined to keeping secrets
- 5. Shapes like curves
- 7. Swollen
- 9. Wide ditch filled with water
- 10. Shook; trembled
- 12. Gladness
- 13. Rose up
- 14. Rubbed
- 15. To one side; awry
- 18. Walked
- 21. Deeply religious; sincere
- 22. Sparkling
- 23. Strong; healthy
- 24. Shallow trenches made in the ground by a plow

Down
- 1. Lacking clear or distinct form
- 3. Recuperating from illness or injury
- 4. Expressed in greater detail
- 6. Secretly
- 8. Splash
- 10. Promised solemnly; pledged
- 11. Small open boat; rowboat
- 12. Moved aimlessly and idly
- 15. Suddenly; without warning
- 16. Walk leisurely
- 17. Tilted
- 19. Goad to action
- 20. Spoke in a monotonous tone

Homecoming Vocabulary Crossword 2

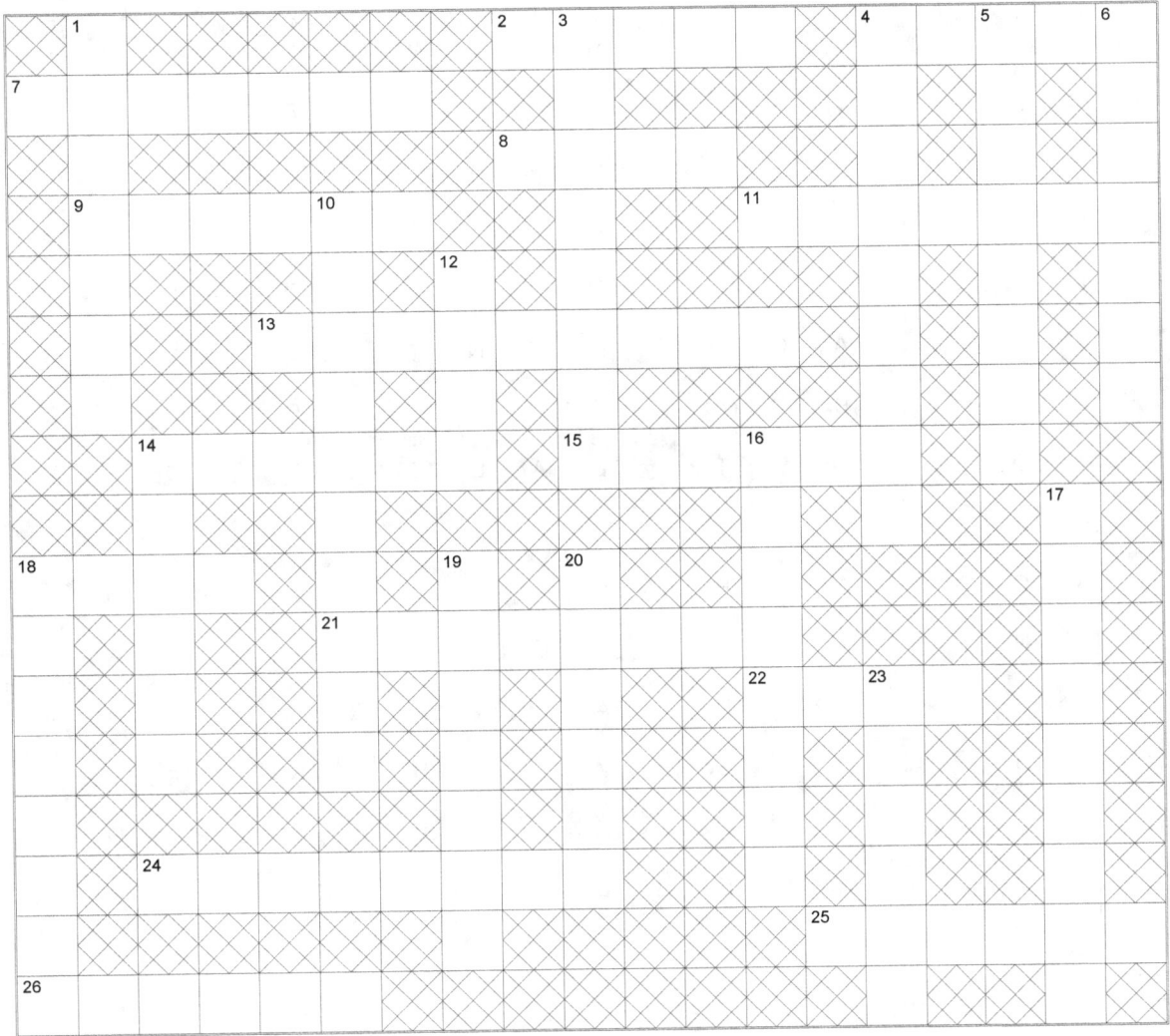

Across
2. To one side; awry
4. Gladness
7. Shallow trenches made in the ground by a plow
8. Deep, prolonged unconsciousness
9. Soothed
11. Slight
13. Jarring, discordant sound
14. Deeply religious; sincere
15. Splash
18. Goad to action
21. Crowded together
22. Shapes like curves
24. Became less
25. Tilted
26. Small open boat; rowboat

Down
1. Put down forcibly
3. Drooped
4. Moved aimlessly and idly
5. Turned; rotated
6. Raised; lifted
10. Expressed in greater detail
12. Wide ditch filled with water
14. Spoke in a monotonous tone
16. Obedient; docile
17. Given up; left behind
18. Beat
19. In a quick, energetic way
20. Bit; chewed on
23. Exulted loudly; boasted

Homecoming Vocabulary Crossword 2 Answer Key

	1 Q					2 A	3 S	K	E	W		4 M	I	5 R	T	6 H
7 F	U	R	R	O	W	S						E		E		O
	E						8 C	O	M	A		A		V		I
	9 L	U	10 L	L	E	D		U			11 T	E	N	U	O	U	S
	L		L			12 M		C				D		L		T
	E		13 C	A	C	O	P	H	O	N	Y		E		V		E
	D			B		A		E					R		E		D
		14 D	E	V	O	U	T		15 D	A	B	16 B	L	E	D		
		R		R								I		D		17 A	
18 P	R	O	D		A		19 B		20 G			D				B	
U		N		21 T	H	R	O	N	G	E	D					A	
M		E		E		I			A		22 A	R	23 C	S		N	
M		D		D		S			W		B		R			D	
E						K			E		L		O			O	
L		24 D	W	I	N	D	L	E	D		E		W			N	
E						Y					25 H	E	E	L	E	D	
26 D	I	N	G	H	Y						D					D	

Across
2. To one side; awry
4. Gladness
7. Shallow trenches made in the ground by a plow
8. Deep, prolonged unconsciousness
9. Soothed
11. Slight
13. Jarring, discordant sound
14. Deeply religious; sincere
15. Splash
18. Goad to action
21. Crowded together
22. Shapes like curves
24. Became less
25. Tilted
26. Small open boat; rowboat

Down
1. Put down forcibly
3. Drooped
4. Moved aimlessly and idly
5. Turned; rotated
6. Raised; lifted
10. Expressed in greater detail
12. Wide ditch filled with water
14. Spoke in a monotonous tone
16. Obedient; docile
17. Given up; left behind
18. Beat
19. In a quick, energetic way
20. Bit; chewed on
23. Exulted loudly; boasted

Homecoming Vocabulary Crossword 3

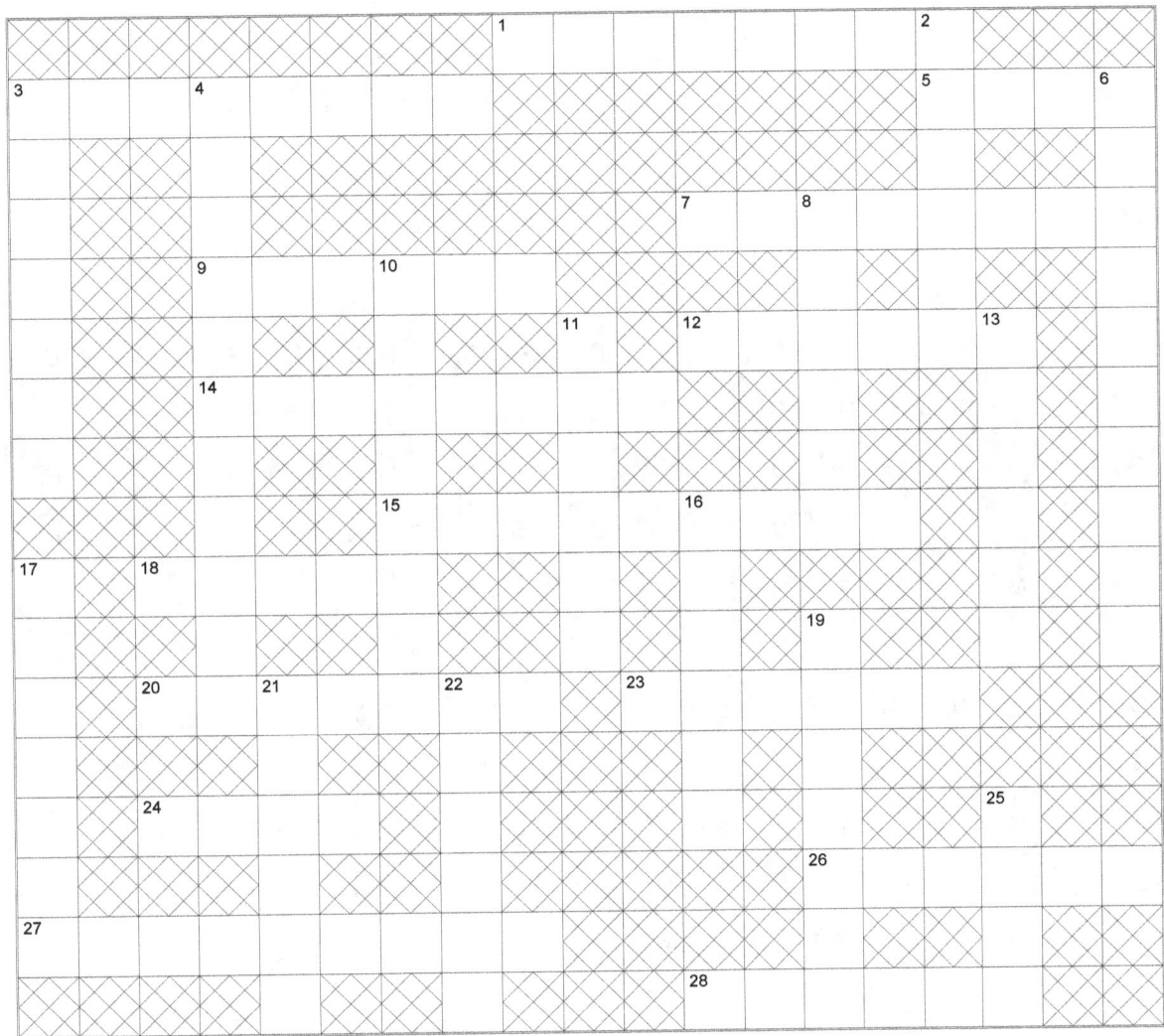

Across
1. Became less
3. Walking laboriously
5. Shapes like curves
7. Unmoving; fixed
9. Puckered
12. Rose up
14. Turned; rotated
15. Jarring, discordant sound
18. Gladness
20. Outrageous
23. Loud outcry
24. Wide ditch filled with water
26. Strong; healthy
27. Came after
28. Rubbed

Down
2. Splash
3. Swarming
4. Despair
6. Secretly
8. Made liquid and glowing
10. Drooped
11. Deeply religious; sincere
13. Small open boat; rowboat
16. Tilted
17. Signs
19. Loss of memory
21. Bit; chewed on
22. Soothed
25. Goad to action

Homecoming Vocabulary Crossword 3 Answer Key

```
                        D W I N D L E D
 T R U D G I N G                A R C S
 E   E                          B     T
 E   S              I M M O B I L E
 M   P U R S E D        O   L     A
 I   E     L      D   W E L L E D L
 N   R E V O L V E D  T       I   T
 G   A     U      V   E       N   H
     T     C A C O P H O N Y  G   I
 S   M I R T H    U   E       H   L
 I   O     E      T   A       Y   Y
 G   U N G O D L Y  C L A M O R
 N   N     U        E   N
 A   M O A T L      D   E   P
 L   W     L            S T U R D Y
 S U C C E E D E D      I   O
     D     D        C H A F E D
```

Across
1. Became less
3. Walking laboriously
5. Shapes like curves
7. Unmoving; fixed
9. Puckered
12. Rose up
14. Turned; rotated
15. Jarring, discordant sound
18. Gladness
20. Outrageous
23. Loud outcry
24. Wide ditch filled with water
26. Strong; healthy
27. Came after
28. Rubbed

Down
2. Splash
3. Swarming
4. Despair
6. Secretly
8. Made liquid and glowing
10. Drooped
11. Deeply religious; sincere
13. Small open boat; rowboat
16. Tilted
17. Signs
19. Loss of memory
21. Bit; chewed on
22. Soothed
25. Goad to action

Homecoming Vocabulary Crossword 4

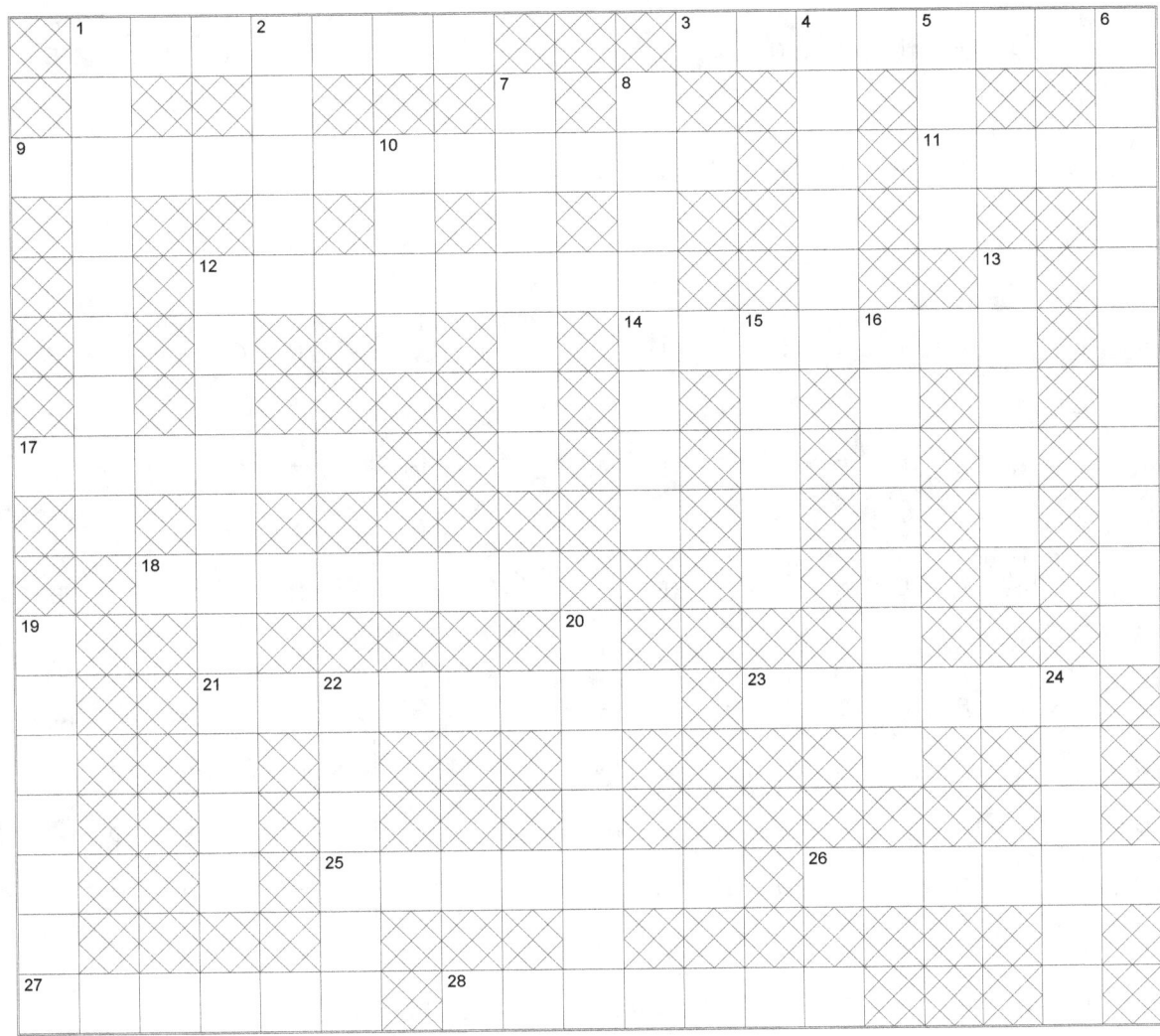

Across
1. Swarming
3. Obedient; docile
9. Distributed randomly among
11. Deep, prolonged unconsciousness
12. Crowded together
14. State of musing; daydream
17. Puckered
18. Walk leisurely
21. Set apart
23. Tilted
25. Shallow trenches made in the ground by a plow
26. Concentrated; firmly fixed
27. Moved up quickly; swelled
28. Hurried along

Down
1. Holding firm; stubborn
2. Gladness
4. Splash
5. Shapes like curves
6. Impatient
7. Delicate; easily broken
8. Twisting, threadlike shoots of a plant
10. Goad to action
12. Invading property or space of another
13. Rose up
15. Promised solemnly; pledged
16. Slow in development
19. Rough-sounding; harsh
20. Slight
22. Rubbed
24. Spoke in a monotonous tone

Homecoming Vocabulary Crossword 4 Answer Key

Across
1. Swarming
3. Obedient; docile
9. Distributed randomly among
11. Deep, prolonged unconsciousness
12. Crowded together
14. State of musing; daydream
17. Puckered
18. Walk leisurely
21. Set apart
23. Tilted
25. Shallow trenches made in the ground by a plow
26. Concentrated; firmly fixed
27. Moved up quickly; swelled
28. Hurried along

Down
1. Holding firm; stubborn
2. Gladness
4. Splash
5. Shapes like curves
6. Impatient
7. Delicate; easily broken
8. Twisting, threadlike shoots of a plant
10. Goad to action
12. Invading property or space of another
13. Rose up
15. Promised solemnly; pledged
16. Slow in development
19. Rough-sounding; harsh
20. Slight
22. Rubbed
24. Spoke in a monotonous tone

Homecoming Vocabulary Juggle Letters 1

1. ONDEBAADN = 1. _____
   Given up; left behind

2. TMAO = 2. _____
   Wide ditch filled with water

3. NOLBIBBG = 3. _____
   Moving about jerkily

4. RBVTEADI = 4. _____
   Shook; trembled

5. TAPONSDREIE = 5. _____
   Despair

6. RYACTRODCONIT = 6. _____
   Opposite of

7. ENTINT = 7. _____
   Concentrated; firmly fixed

8. UNSTERA = 8. _____
   Walk leisurely

9. SRAEIPTD = 9. _____
   Walked

10. BEILDDAB = 10. _____
    Obedient; docile

11. EHTISDO = 11. _____
    Raised; lifted

12. COMRLA = 12. _____
    Loud outcry

13. CUNSEFLO = 13. _____
    Gathered material attached to a skirt

14. TAERHYRDEI = 14. _____
    Genetically transmitted

15. RJUETNCCOE = 15. _____
    Guesswork

Homecoming Vocabulary Juggle Letters 1 Answer Key

1. ONDEBAADN = 1. ABANDONED
Given up; left behind

2. TMAO = 2. MOAT
Wide ditch filled with water

3. NOLBIBBG = 3. BOBBLING
Moving about jerkily

4. RBVTEADI = 4. VIBRATED
Shook; trembled

5. TAPONSDREIE = 5. DESPERATION
Despair

6. RYACTRODCONIT = 6. CONTRADICTORY
Opposite of

7. ENTINT = 7. INTENT
Concentrated; firmly fixed

8. UNSTERA = 8. SAUNTER
Walk leisurely

9. SRAEIPTD = 9. TRAIPSED
Walked

10. BEILDDAB =10. BIDDABLE
Obedient; docile

11. EHTISDO =11. HOISTED
Raised; lifted

12. COMRLA =12. CLAMOR
Loud outcry

13. CUNSEFLO =13. FLOUNCES
Gathered material attached to a skirt

14. TAERHYRDEI =14. HEREDITARY
Genetically transmitted

15. RJUETNCCOE =15. CONJECTURE
Guesswork

Homecoming Vocabulary Juggle Letters 2

1. STEDLOU = 1. _____
   Rumpled; disheveled

2. RTHMI = 2. _____
   Gladness

3. LBABED = 3. _____
   Splash

4. NTRPRDEESEIS = 4. _____
   Distributed randomly among

5. BNBLOIGB = 5. _____
   Moving about jerkily

6. LRILTE = 6. _____
   Lever that steers the boat

7. DEUELLQ = 7. _____
   Put down forcibly

8. ARNSEEOIPTD = 8. _____
   Despair

9. LIFAREG = 9. _____
   Delicate; easily broken

10. IRNITEGC = 10. _____
    Repeating

11. UDSGER = 11. _____
    Moved up quickly; swelled

12. DLEGMAE = 12. _____
    Glowed

13. ATORCYRN = 13. _____
    Willful; perverse; ornery

14. CUCTISROIU = 14. _____
    Roundabout

15. MMYTSEYR = 15. _____
    Balanced or harmonious proportions

Homecoming Vocabulary Juggle Letters 2 Answer Key

1. STEDLOU = 1. TOUSLED
Rumpled; disheveled

2. RTHMI = 2. MIRTH
Gladness

3. LBABED = 3. DABBLE
Splash

4. NTRPRDEESEIS = 4. INTERSPERSED
Distributed randomly among

5. BNBLOIGB = 5. BOBBLING
Moving about jerkily

6. LRILTE = 6. TILLER
Lever that steers the boat

7. DEUELLQ = 7. QUELLED
Put down forcibly

8. ARNSEEOIPTD = 8. DESPERATION
Despair

9. LIFAREG = 9. FRAGILE
Delicate; easily broken

10. IRNITEGC =10. RECITING
Repeating

11. UDSGER =11. SURGED
Moved up quickly; swelled

12. DLEGMAE =12. GLEAMED
Glowed

13. ATORCYRN =13. CONTRARY
Willful; perverse; ornery

14. CUCTISROIU =14. CIRCUITOUS
Roundabout

15. MMYTSEYR =15. SYMMETRY
Balanced or harmonious proportions

Homecoming Vocabulary Juggle Letters 3

1. ABRTLDAEOE = 1. _____
   Expressed in greater detail

2. GUERDS = 2. _____
   Moved up quickly; swelled

3. EOCSDULH = 3. _____
   Drooped

4. DEHLEE = 4. _____
   Tilted

5. NILASGS = 5. _____
   Signs

6. ORCMAL = 6. _____
   Loud outcry

7. SUTCOIIRCU = 7. _____
   Roundabout

8. CDUEESLD = 8. _____
   Set apart

9. RNATAYSCU = 9. _____
   Place of refuge

10. TAREDEDR =10. _____
    Slow in development

11. LEUDQEL =11. _____
    Put down forcibly

12. LRYABTUP =12. _____
    Suddenly; without warning

13. AMDGEEL =13. _____
    Glowed

14. ASUUOCR =14. _____
    Rough-sounding; harsh

15. DRAYONG =15. _____
    Stiff fabric of cotton or silk

Homecoming Vocabulary Juggle Letters 3 Answer Key

1. ABRTLDAEOE = 1. ELABORATED
Expressed in greater detail

2. GUERDS = 2. SURGED
Moved up quickly; swelled

3. EOCSDULH = 3. SLOUCHED
Drooped

4. DEHLEE = 4. HEELED
Tilted

5. NILASGS = 5. SIGNALS
Signs

6. ORCMAL = 6. CLAMOR
Loud outcry

7. SUTCOIIRCU = 7. CIRCUITOUS
Roundabout

8. CDUEESLD = 8. SECLUDED
Set apart

9. RNATAYSCU = 9. SANCTUARY
Place of refuge

10. TAREDEDR =10. RETARDED
Slow in development

11. LEUDQEL =11. QUELLED
Put down forcibly

12. LRYABTUP =12. ABRUPTLY
Suddenly; without warning

13. AMDGEEL =13. GLEAMED
Glowed

14. ASUUOCR =14. RAUCOUS
Rough-sounding; harsh

15. DRAYONG =15. ORGANDY
Stiff fabric of cotton or silk

Homecoming Vocabulary Juggle Letters 4

1. SIERPTGANSS = 1. _____
   Invading property or space of another

2. ETDOISH = 2. _____
   Raised; lifted

3. UOCITCRUIS = 3. _____
   Roundabout

4. OELMTN = 4. _____
   Made liquid and glowing

5. AUGYHNT = 5. _____
   Mischievous

6. MMEDULEP = 6. _____
   Beat

7. OSIGNOTPNP = 7. _____
   Putting off until a later time

8. USWFORR = 8. _____
   Shallow trenches made in the ground by a plow

9. OETGHRND = 9. _____
   Crowded together

10. MYRLIP =10. _____
    Properly; precisely

11. EEEIRRV =11. _____
    State of musing; daydream

12. ATBSARE =12. _____
    Side by side

13. HMTRI =13. _____
    Gladness

14. YNRDGOA =14. _____
    Stiff fabric of cotton or silk

15. SOEUNTU =15. _____
    Slight

Homecoming Vocabulary Juggle Letters 4 Answer Key

1. SIERPTGANSS = 1. TRESPASSING
Invading property or space of another

2. ETDOISH = 2. HOISTED
Raised; lifted

3. UOCITCRUIS = 3. CIRCUITOUS
Roundabout

4. OELMTN = 4. MOLTEN
Made liquid and glowing

5. AUGYHNT = 5. NAUGHTY
Mischievous

6. MMEDULEP = 6. PUMMELED
Beat

7. OSIGNOTPNP = 7. POSTPONING
Putting off until a later time

8. USWFORR = 8. FURROWS
Shallow trenches made in the ground by a plow

9. OETGHRND = 9. THRONGED
Crowded together

10. MYRLIP = 10. PRIMLY
Properly; precisely

11. EEEIRRV = 11. REVERIE
State of musing; daydream

12. ATBSARE = 12. ABREAST
Side by side

13. HMTRI = 13. MIRTH
Gladness

14. YNRDGOA = 14. ORGANDY
Stiff fabric of cotton or silk

15. SOEUNTU = 15. TENUOUS
Slight

ABANDONED	Given up; left behind
ABREAST	Side by side
ABRUPTLY	Suddenly; without warning
AMNESIA	Loss of memory
ARCS	Shapes like curves
ASKEW	To one side; awry
BICKERING	Squabbling; having little quarrels

BIDDABLE	Obedient; docile
BOBBLING	Moving about jerkily
BRISKLY	In a quick, energetic way
CACOPHONY	Jarring, discordant sound
CHAFED	Rubbed
CIRCUITOUS	Roundabout
CLAMOR	Loud outcry

CLENCHED	Closed tightly
COCOON	Comfortable retreat; refuge
COMA	Deep, prolonged unconsciousness
CONJECTURE	Guesswork
CONSPICUOUS	Obvious
CONTRADICTORY	Opposite of
CONTRARY	Willful; perverse; ornery

CONVALESCENT	Recuperating from illness or injury
CONVICTION	Strong belief or opinion
CROWED	Exulted loudly; boasted
DABBLE	Splash
DESPERATION	Despair
DEVOUT	Deeply religious; sincere
DINGHY	Small open boat; rowboat

DRONED	Spoke in a monotonous tone
DWINDLED	Became less
ELABORATED	Expressed in greater detail
EXASPERATED	Impatient
FALTERED	Weakened; became unsteady
FATIGUE	Weariness; exhaustion
FLOUNCES	Gathered material attached to a skirt

FLUSTERED	Made nervous or upset
FRAGILE	Delicate; easily broken
FURROWS	Shallow trenches made in the ground by a plow
GLEAMED	Glowed
GLIMPSE	See briefly
GLINTING	Sparkling
GNAWED	Bit; chewed on

GURGLED	Make a kind of bubbling sound
HEELED	Tilted
HEREDITARY	Genetically transmitted
HOISTED	Raised; lifted
HUSTLED	Hurried along
IMMOBILE	Unmoving; fixed
INTENT	Concentrated; firmly fixed

INTERSPERSED	Distributed randomly among
LULLED	Soothed
MEANDERED	Moved aimlessly and idly
MIRTH	Gladness
MOAT	Wide ditch filled with water
MOLTEN	Made liquid and glowing
MOURNFUL	Causing or suggesting sadness

NAUGHTY	Mischievous
ORGANDY	Stiff fabric of cotton or silk
POSTPONING	Putting off until a later time
PRIMLY	Properly; precisely
PROD	Goad to action
PUMMELED	Beat
PURSED	Puckered

QUELLED	Put down forcibly
RAUCOUS	Rough-sounding; harsh
RECITING	Repeating
RETARDED	Slow in development
REVERIE	State of musing; daydream
REVOLVED	Turned; rotated
SANCTUARY	Place of refuge

SAUNTER	Walk leisurely
SCOWLED	Frowned
SECLUDED	Set apart
SECRETIVE	Inclined to keeping secrets
SIGNALS	Signs
SLOUCHED	Drooped
SOLEMNLY	Somberly; earnestly

SOLITUDE	State of being alone
STEALTHILY	Secretly
STURDY	Strong; healthy
SUCCEEDED	Came after
SURGED	Moved up quickly; swelled
SYMMETRY	Balanced or harmonious proportions
TEEMING	Swarming

TENACIOUS	Holding firm; stubborn
TENDRILS	Twisting, threadlike shoots of a plant
TENUOUS	Slight
THRONGED	Crowded together
TILLER	Lever that steers the boat
TOUSLED	Rumpled; disheveled
TRAIPSED	Walked

TRESPASSING	Invading property or space of another
TRUDGING	Walking laboriously
TURGID	Swollen
UNGODLY	Outrageous
VAGUE	Lacking clear or distinct form
VIBRATED	Shook; trembled
VOWED	Promised solemnly; pledged

WELLED	Rose up
ZIGZAG	Make sharp turns in alternating directions

Homecoming Vocabulary

TURGID	HOISTED	SECRETIVE	SAUNTER	QUELLED
CHAFED	EXASPERATED	UNGODLY	TEEMING	GLEAMED
BIDDABLE	THRONGED	FREE SPACE	COMA	SOLEMNLY
TRAIPSED	SOLITUDE	FURROWS	PUMMELED	SIGNALS
TRUDGING	REVOLVED	FLOUNCES	SYMMETRY	ABANDONED

Homecoming Vocabulary

TRESPASSING	TENUOUS	STEALTHILY	IMMOBILE	CLENCHED
SURGED	GNAWED	DEVOUT	DESPERATION	CONSPICUOUS
HEREDITARY	CACOPHONY	FREE SPACE	COCOON	MOURNFUL
MEANDERED	CONJECTURE	PRIMLY	SCOWLED	FRAGILE
VIBRATED	MIRTH	TENACIOUS	CIRCUITOUS	VOWED

Homecoming Vocabulary

GURGLED	REVOLVED	CIRCUITOUS	TOUSLED	EXASPERATED
SCOWLED	FALTERED	SAUNTER	FRAGILE	HEREDITARY
COMA	ASKEW	FREE SPACE	HEELED	CLENCHED
POSTPONING	CONTRADICTORY	GLIMPSE	PURSED	LULLED
FURROWS	RAUCOUS	TENUOUS	ZIGZAG	ABRUPTLY

Homecoming Vocabulary

GNAWED	PROD	STURDY	INTENT	VOWED
IMMOBILE	DABBLE	THRONGED	TURGID	MEANDERED
CHAFED	TRUDGING	FREE SPACE	MOLTEN	TRESPASSING
CROWED	VIBRATED	MIRTH	TRAIPSED	DESPERATION
DRONED	GLEAMED	INTERSPERSED	QUELLED	COCOON

Homecoming Vocabulary

TENDRILS	DRONED	VIBRATED	HEELED	POSTPONING
STEALTHILY	CIRCUITOUS	FRAGILE	CONVALESCENT	CACOPHONY
SIGNALS	TILLER	FREE SPACE	COCOON	SOLITUDE
EXASPERATED	UNGODLY	GURGLED	CONSPICUOUS	CLENCHED
TRESPASSING	RETARDED	THRONGED	CHAFED	DWINDLED

Homecoming Vocabulary

ZIGZAG	TRUDGING	SANCTUARY	PRIMLY	ARCS
ELABORATED	CLAMOR	CONVICTION	SECLUDED	GLINTING
MOLTEN	ASKEW	FREE SPACE	SECRETIVE	RECITING
PROD	DABBLE	DESPERATION	FALTERED	IMMOBILE
TENUOUS	QUELLED	FLOUNCES	TENACIOUS	VAGUE

Homecoming Vocabulary

COCOON	UNGODLY	SOLEMNLY	PROD	GURGLED
INTERSPERSED	CONTRADICTORY	SCOWLED	TURGID	EXASPERATED
FRAGILE	REVERIE	FREE SPACE	BICKERING	CACOPHONY
TENUOUS	PRIMLY	HEELED	STEALTHILY	DESPERATION
GNAWED	DABBLE	MOLTEN	ELABORATED	LULLED

Homecoming Vocabulary

MOURNFUL	SOLITUDE	ABREAST	WELLED	FATIGUE
CONVALESCENT	PUMMELED	CONJECTURE	CLENCHED	VIBRATED
VOWED	DRONED	FREE SPACE	RAUCOUS	SLOUCHED
GLEAMED	INTENT	FALTERED	SIGNALS	DEVOUT
POSTPONING	DINGHY	GLIMPSE	BIDDABLE	QUELLED

Homecoming Vocabulary

DESPERATION	ARCS	SLOUCHED	SURGED	RETARDED
DEVOUT	TRAIPSED	HEREDITARY	ABRUPTLY	BIDDABLE
ABREAST	FLUSTERED	FREE SPACE	REVERIE	TENDRILS
CROWED	QUELLED	MOLTEN	GURGLED	UNGODLY
BRISKLY	SECRETIVE	ZIGZAG	GLIMPSE	PROD

Homecoming Vocabulary

FRAGILE	SECLUDED	BOBBLING	AMNESIA	GLINTING
SUCCEEDED	INTERSPERSED	RECITING	VAGUE	MEANDERED
RAUCOUS	HUSTLED	FREE SPACE	SOLEMNLY	CLENCHED
TENACIOUS	CONTRARY	TRUDGING	SOLITUDE	POSTPONING
STEALTHILY	MOAT	GNAWED	CLAMOR	LULLED

Homecoming Vocabulary

REVERIE	SLOUCHED	ABREAST	POSTPONING	MOURNFUL
DRONED	INTERSPERSED	ELABORATED	FALTERED	TRAIPSED
DWINDLED	CHAFED	FREE SPACE	CROWED	FLOUNCES
CACOPHONY	NAUGHTY	BOBBLING	DESPERATION	SUCCEEDED
FRAGILE	SECRETIVE	GLEAMED	ARCS	CLAMOR

Homecoming Vocabulary

SOLEMNLY	DEVOUT	SAUNTER	CONJECTURE	SIGNALS
CONVICTION	STEALTHILY	ABANDONED	TILLER	CONVALESCENT
PROD	AMNESIA	FREE SPACE	VAGUE	MIRTH
FLUSTERED	GURGLED	TEEMING	RETARDED	HUSTLED
WELLED	ABRUPTLY	GNAWED	RECITING	COCOON

Homecoming Vocabulary

CONJECTURE	ZIGZAG	BOBBLING	CONTRADICTORY	HEREDITARY
SOLEMNLY	BRISKLY	MEANDERED	INTERSPERSED	RETARDED
RAUCOUS	GURGLED	FREE SPACE	SURGED	SECRETIVE
SANCTUARY	CACOPHONY	ABRUPTLY	TENUOUS	TRUDGING
COMA	GLIMPSE	ELABORATED	SYMMETRY	SLOUCHED

Homecoming Vocabulary

GNAWED	ABANDONED	INTENT	SCOWLED	WELLED
CLENCHED	TENDRILS	PRIMLY	EXASPERATED	SOLITUDE
IMMOBILE	DABBLE	FREE SPACE	CIRCUITOUS	SAUNTER
PROD	TURGID	ORGANDY	TEEMING	TOUSLED
FRAGILE	FURROWS	FALTERED	SECLUDED	UNGODLY

Homecoming Vocabulary

MOLTEN	ELABORATED	CROWED	REVERIE	GNAWED
DWINDLED	ABRUPTLY	DABBLE	CLAMOR	TURGID
PROD	TEEMING	FREE SPACE	AMNESIA	CONVALESCENT
RECITING	RETARDED	THRONGED	ORGANDY	WELLED
TILLER	BICKERING	SLOUCHED	FATIGUE	BOBBLING

Homecoming Vocabulary

CONTRADICTORY	EXASPERATED	CLENCHED	SANCTUARY	TENUOUS
STEALTHILY	GLIMPSE	PRIMLY	DEVOUT	MIRTH
CONTRARY	GLEAMED	FREE SPACE	SOLEMNLY	SURGED
ZIGZAG	SCOWLED	HEELED	BIDDABLE	PURSED
INTERSPERSED	STURDY	ARCS	TENACIOUS	HOISTED

Homecoming Vocabulary

BOBBLING	FATIGUE	COMA	BIDDABLE	CONTRARY
AMNESIA	REVOLVED	SECRETIVE	FLOUNCES	DABBLE
DINGHY	LULLED	FREE SPACE	CACOPHONY	FALTERED
TENDRILS	UNGODLY	TENUOUS	CONJECTURE	SOLITUDE
SUCCEEDED	PURSED	CROWED	BICKERING	DESPERATION

Homecoming Vocabulary

WELLED	ASKEW	MOAT	TURGID	EXASPERATED
SLOUCHED	CONVICTION	ABRUPTLY	CONTRADICTORY	NAUGHTY
GLEAMED	CONSPICUOUS	FREE SPACE	POSTPONING	HEELED
VIBRATED	INTERSPERSED	TRAIPSED	SECLUDED	FRAGILE
SOLEMNLY	SANCTUARY	VAGUE	REVERIE	MIRTH

Homecoming Vocabulary

TRUDGING	MOAT	STEALTHILY	CLENCHED	REVOLVED
RETARDED	UNGODLY	PRIMLY	STURDY	BIDDABLE
MIRTH	CIRCUITOUS	FREE SPACE	CONTRADICTORY	TENUOUS
CLAMOR	HOISTED	VAGUE	MOURNFUL	SANCTUARY
PUMMELED	SIGNALS	SOLEMNLY	GLIMPSE	CROWED

Homecoming Vocabulary

TILLER	SECRETIVE	INTENT	GLEAMED	RECITING
TURGID	SURGED	VIBRATED	WELLED	BOBBLING
AMNESIA	HUSTLED	FREE SPACE	REVERIE	PROD
TENDRILS	IMMOBILE	MOLTEN	ABREAST	RAUCOUS
NAUGHTY	PURSED	TRAIPSED	SYMMETRY	FLUSTERED

Homecoming Vocabulary

VOWED	SIGNALS	CROWED	CLENCHED	DWINDLED
HEELED	ASKEW	CONSPICUOUS	THRONGED	PRIMLY
CLAMOR	BRISKLY	FREE SPACE	TRESPASSING	HEREDITARY
PROD	MEANDERED	ABRUPTLY	FRAGILE	FALTERED
REVERIE	FLOUNCES	TURGID	SOLITUDE	REVOLVED

Homecoming Vocabulary

PUMMELED	GNAWED	GLINTING	RECITING	VAGUE
SAUNTER	SLOUCHED	GLEAMED	VIBRATED	RAUCOUS
STEALTHILY	BICKERING	FREE SPACE	LULLED	CONVALESCENT
SYMMETRY	TEEMING	DINGHY	TRUDGING	ABREAST
FURROWS	STURDY	AMNESIA	NAUGHTY	CONTRARY

Homecoming Vocabulary

ORGANDY	CLENCHED	MIRTH	HUSTLED	DABBLE
FLOUNCES	SECRETIVE	CONSPICUOUS	TRUDGING	HEREDITARY
TRESPASSING	DINGHY	FREE SPACE	ABREAST	TRAIPSED
REVOLVED	ARCS	PRIMLY	PUMMELED	BOBBLING
EXASPERATED	COCOON	FATIGUE	GNAWED	STEALTHILY

Homecoming Vocabulary

TURGID	SUCCEEDED	CACOPHONY	CONJECTURE	IMMOBILE
FALTERED	CIRCUITOUS	REVERIE	ASKEW	BICKERING
FURROWS	PURSED	FREE SPACE	GURGLED	AMNESIA
ELABORATED	SIGNALS	INTERSPERSED	DWINDLED	TOUSLED
MEANDERED	BIDDABLE	MOAT	CHAFED	UNGODLY

Homecoming Vocabulary

COMA	SOLITUDE	TENDRILS	SECLUDED	WELLED
CACOPHONY	SURGED	TOUSLED	SCOWLED	BOBBLING
QUELLED	TURGID	FREE SPACE	NAUGHTY	RECITING
POSTPONING	CLENCHED	HUSTLED	PUMMELED	SECRETIVE
ELABORATED	THRONGED	SAUNTER	SUCCEEDED	TRESPASSING

Homecoming Vocabulary

BRISKLY	PRIMLY	CONJECTURE	SOLEMNLY	REVOLVED
TENUOUS	MEANDERED	PROD	GNAWED	HOISTED
TRAIPSED	RETARDED	FREE SPACE	FLUSTERED	DWINDLED
CLAMOR	SLOUCHED	VAGUE	ZIGZAG	CROWED
INTERSPERSED	PURSED	CONVICTION	GLEAMED	ARCS

Homecoming Vocabulary

GLIMPSE	STURDY	SUCCEEDED	DEVOUT	DINGHY
SANCTUARY	TRESPASSING	ZIGZAG	CONTRARY	QUELLED
SOLITUDE	GNAWED	FREE SPACE	RAUCOUS	CLAMOR
COMA	SAUNTER	BOBBLING	PURSED	POSTPONING
SYMMETRY	ABRUPTLY	SIGNALS	SECRETIVE	REVERIE

Homecoming Vocabulary

VAGUE	TENUOUS	BRISKLY	HEREDITARY	TILLER
CLENCHED	TRUDGING	FATIGUE	SLOUCHED	CACOPHONY
PRIMLY	TENACIOUS	FREE SPACE	CHAFED	WELLED
REVOLVED	DABBLE	DESPERATION	GURGLED	CIRCUITOUS
HUSTLED	AMNESIA	SCOWLED	CONVICTION	BIDDABLE

Homecoming Vocabulary

SECLUDED	TEEMING	DABBLE	PRIMLY	VIBRATED
SUCCEEDED	COMA	REVERIE	INTERSPERSED	FATIGUE
SIGNALS	STURDY	FREE SPACE	GURGLED	GLIMPSE
AMNESIA	CONTRADICTORY	MEANDERED	TOUSLED	IMMOBILE
PROD	GNAWED	SECRETIVE	DRONED	FURROWS

Homecoming Vocabulary

TRUDGING	CHAFED	RETARDED	CACOPHONY	ELABORATED
BIDDABLE	ABREAST	VOWED	SLOUCHED	UNGODLY
FLUSTERED	ARCS	FREE SPACE	TILLER	RAUCOUS
SCOWLED	REVOLVED	CLAMOR	WELLED	MIRTH
FALTERED	VAGUE	SAUNTER	SYMMETRY	ABANDONED

Homecoming Vocabulary

VAGUE	SIGNALS	VIBRATED	INTERSPERSED	ABANDONED
AMNESIA	REVERIE	HUSTLED	DWINDLED	TURGID
TRUDGING	CROWED	FREE SPACE	CONJECTURE	SOLITUDE
THRONGED	STURDY	POSTPONING	COCOON	SURGED
TENDRILS	FATIGUE	FRAGILE	GNAWED	SCOWLED

Homecoming Vocabulary

GLEAMED	WELLED	SLOUCHED	MEANDERED	TOUSLED
FLOUNCES	RECITING	FLUSTERED	CIRCUITOUS	TRAIPSED
ABRUPTLY	TRESPASSING	FREE SPACE	ZIGZAG	TENACIOUS
CONTRARY	VOWED	DINGHY	PRIMLY	ORGANDY
HEELED	INTENT	SECLUDED	PROD	PUMMELED